Kristen Lang

Creative Redemption

D1807400

Kristen Lang

Creative Redemption

Uncertainty in Poetic Creativity

VDM Verlag Dr. Müller

Imprint

Bibliographic information by the German National Library: The German National Library lists this publication at the German National Bibliography; detailed bibliographic information is available on the Internet at http://dnb.d-nb.de.

Any brand names and product names mentioned in this book are subject to trademark, brand or patent protection and are trademarks or registered trademarks of their respective holders. The use of brand names, product names, common names, trade names, product descriptions etc. even without a particular marking in this works is in no way to be construed to mean that such names may be regarded as unrestricted in respect of trademark and brand protection legislation and could thus be used by anyone.

Cover image: www.purestockx.com

Publisher:
VDM Verlag Dr. Müller Aktiengesellschaft & Co. KG , Dudweiler Landstr. 125 a, 66123 Saarbrücken, Germany,
Phone +49 681 9100-698, Fax +49 681 9100-988,
Email: info@vdm-verlag.de

Zugl.: Geelong, Deakin University, Diss., 2004

Produced in USA and UK by:
Lightning Source Inc., La Vergne, Tennessee, USA
Lightning Source UK Ltd., Milton Keynes, UK
BookSurge LLC, 5341 Dorchester Road, Suite 16, North Charleston, SC 29418, USA

ISBN: 978-3-639-05590-0

To balance on the ridge

Acknowledgements

Thanks to Dr David McCooey for his valued support in the development of this project, and to Deakin University for ideal conditions. Thanks, also, to the Australian Government and the Deakin University Board for making available the Australian Postgraduate Award with which the writing was funded. Thanks, further, to Laurie, Judy and Michael for everything else.

Contents:

Prologue   5

Introduction

❖ Language and Experience   7
   Interlude: Language
              Communiqué   13
❖ Creative Redemption   14
   Interlude: Redemption
              Song   18
❖ Contractuality – an Overview   19

Intermission: Uncertainty
              hieroglyphic   21
              Bartering with a young child   22
              Gap: 23
              Language   23
              Making Our Minds Up   24
              Sure   25
              relativity   26

Section I: Translation

❖ The Treachery of Language   27
   Interlude: Never Hitting the Mark
              Blue Balloon   30
              Up   31
❖ Uncertainty   32
   Interlude: Approaching Certainty
              Love on a Shoreline   37
❖ Persuasion   39
   Interlude: Provocative Lies
              Caving: a translation   42
❖ Conclusion   43

Intermission: Translation
              Night Swim   44
              Aurora   45

cello concerto   45

Painting, 1810   46

intimacy   47

Beside me   47

Threading the moon   48

Ligeti, smiling   50

Section II: Constraints

❖ The Form of Freedom   51

Interlude: Taking Shape

    Faith   54

❖ The Act of Writing   55

Interlude: Emerging Patterns

    flow   59

    in no mood   60

❖ Cross-discipline Constraints   62

Interlude: Jazz

    The Line   65

❖ Constraints and Redemption   66

Interlude: Irresponsibility

    sound   69

❖ Conclusion   70

Intermission: Playing with Form

    Postcard   72

    Six Wishes   73

    Postcard   74

    Doubt   74

    Wait   74

    Arrival   74

    Want   75

    (Ul)tim(at)ely   75

    Trust takes its chances   76

    A20   76

    Number Storm   77

    A Word from Mathematics   78

    Algebra   79

    Postcards   79

    Milling   80

Section III: Appeal

❖ Aesthetic Constraints   81
    Interlude: Idealism
        To call ourselves modern   83
❖ A Unique Repetition   84
    Interlude: Be Me But Not Me
        Tenacity   87
❖ Contextual Idealism   88
    Interlude: Incontestability
        Losing the Dream   90
❖ Redeeming Taste   92
    Interlude: Uncertain Aspirations
        Journeying   94
        internet   94
❖ The Vocation of Poetry   95
    Interlude: Aesthetic Development
        If ardour prospers   100
❖ Conclusion   103

Coda: Creativity – the urge and the act
        Island   105
        Vision   106
        Nautilus   106
        Attaining Wisdom   107
        Revolution   108
        Midnight   108
        Impact   109
        From his room   109
        Symphonic Dance   110
        Redemption   112
        the artist pretends to feel   112
        Behind a poet in the dole queue   113
        Cave Art   113
        tilt   114
        In the middle of things   114
        infringement   115

Endnotes   117
Bibliography   124

Creative Redemption:

Uncertainty in Poetic Creativity

Prologue:

Poetic creativity begins with points of indeterminacy; uncertainty is a condition for its pursuit. What happens if we embrace this as our premise? The notion that a resolution can be attempted and is worth attempting would need to be equally available. The combination would allow the act of writing poetry to be one that promised to redeem a capacity for persuasive, poetic expression. Seeking original expression suited to *this* moment, in *this* place, a poet may wish to break from established responses to uncertainty (i.e., traditions), thereby threatening, in *order* to redeem, that same capacity. Uncertainty and redemption are concerns addressed in the work that follows: what are the relations between them, it is asked, as experienced by creative individuals and by poets in particular. The discussion demands consideration of the exchanges between language, experience, and poetic expression. Responses to Maurice Blanchot, Jacques Derrida, Kevin Hart, and Harold Bloom acknowledge that there is dense integration between the three, but also ineradicable differences. Coherent, poetic effects compromise the experiences poets are informed by, marking the arrival of other experiences and the impossibility of pure translation. Tensions between poets and their precursors are part of what informs the struggle to decide which transmutations might be regarded as worthwhile poetry. The perfect poem is never achieved: no creative act redeems absolutely, for doubt is never entirely removed. Redemption, then, reflects a poet's sense that a surrogate for an impossible promise has been delivered. This surrogate is a poem that allows its author to consider that his or her influence and sensibilities have forged, not certainty itself, but poetic significance. Necessarily, such significance is subjectively judged, in relation to other poems, and in relation to ideas about what poetry may yet become. Poems afford, accordingly, only a tenuous resolution amid uncertainties that are incessantly available, uncertainties that are unsettling, a source, perhaps, of anxiety, but also, within the medium, enabling. Revelation is always possible, though it may always fall to further creativity.

Introduction:

Language and Experience

Condemned to subjectivity in the grip of an intractable world, we are bound to refer to the authority of convention. Using an inherited language, we attempt to build meaningful representations of ourselves and our surroundings. Convention tells us what kinds of descriptions have been effective in the past. It cannot guarantee, however, that what we think and feel will seem to be satisfactorily expressed. Circumstances change, and we do not rely, accordingly, on convention alone. Spurred by the need, or desire, to voice responses peculiar to our time and to ourselves, we arrive at, and employ, individual creativity. Creative influence can be observed as an element of daily thought and speech, and becomes more concentrated in certain fields of work. One of these fields is poetry. A poet attempts to renew existing capacities for expression in ways that are both conventionally poetic and specific to his or her immediate situation. What is it that allows and drives the process? In what follows, relations between language, experience, and poetic expression, the uncertainties these relations invite and the opportunities they offer, are given as answers to this question. But the relations are complex and it is useful, for a number of reasons, to focus firstly on language itself.

We use a language comprised of signs that are, by definition, transferable into any number of expressions and into any number of relations with other signs. Inherently impersonal, these signs embed us in awareness, but also in mediation. Maurice Blanchot, who has written extensively on the relations between language and experience and whose writing is significantly influential in the work that follows, emphasises the duality: "The word gives me the being," Blanchot writes, "but it gives it to me deprived of being".[1] Words are a means of expression, but are also signs that relate primarily to other signs rather than to specific events and feelings. For language to reflect being perfectly, either its signs would need to become so particularised that they would cease to be signs (the language would disappear), or our perceptions of our own being would need to be not partially but wholly conditioned by available terms of expression (nothing could then appear to be new). We live with neither extreme. This realisation marks a further quality of the language we use. The word gives me the being and gives it to me deprived of being because signs are both flexible *and* impersonal. We are neither entirely controlling nor entirely controlled. Formal repetition combines with ongoing and subjective revision. Convention and the potential to extend, thwart, and adjust convention turn out to be part of the same arrangement. The word "gives me the being" because the effects of language can be (and are) repeatedly and subjectively, and sometimes creatively, renewed. The explications that follow for these claims are to a large extent (and happily) Derridean.

What language cannot do is deliver absolute certainty. "Truth, unveiling, illumination are no longer decided in the appropriation of the truth of being," Jacques Derrida writes, "but are cast into its bottomless abyss as non-truth, veiling and dissimulation".[2] He repeats the sentiment in another text: "No one inflection enjoys any absolute privilege, no meaning can be fixed or decided upon. No border is guaranteed, inside or out".[3] Derrida is not suggesting that we are powerless to say anything at all. His work demands, rather, an awareness of the provisionality of interpretative norms, an awareness "that the structure of the machine, or the springs, are not so tight, so that you can just try to dislocate".[4] There is a machine, and one we cannot avoid using, but an aporia of interpretative uncertainty resonates within it. Apparent truth, reasonableness, or legitimacy, can always be deconstructed; interpretative choices and ambiguities can always be exposed. The language we inherit, Derrida argues, is always (and already) a participant in an unrelieved and unresolved relay of signification. Jeremy Hawthorn reiterates that meaning "is always relational, never self-present or self-constituted".[5] Hence, *pure* presence" becomes "chains of differential marks".[6] There are no transcendental signifiers, Derrida writes, only the complexity and contingency of

> substitutive significations which could only come forth in a chain of differential references, the 'real' supervening, and being added only while taking on meaning from a trace and from an invocation of the supplement, etc.[7]

Ceaseless movement ripples across infinite points of comparison, waving at a final signified that is never reached. "The sign", Madan Sarup explains, "must be studied 'under erasure', always already inhabited by the trace of another sign which never appears as such".[8]

Language allows a capacity for expression but cannot secure the source(s) of inspiration for any particular utterance. Complex feelings and ideas can appear to be communicated (this is in itself remarkable), histories can appear to be recorded, but the transition from being into language is not smooth. The relay of signs cannot be traced back to the subjects that seem to be its source: there are only other signs. Being-as-it-is and being-as-it-might-be-represented may reflect each other in passing, but cannot intersect. There is always a gap. Ann Smock, in her introduction to Blanchot's *The Space of Literature*, suggests that a writer seeking complete integrity will find an "inexhaustibly persistent presence of absence".[9] Blanchot offers an analogy: if we stand beside a corpse, there is a sense in which the dead person remains with us while being also, and permanently, not with us.[10] To represent a thing in words, Blanchot means, is to keep it with us while also removing it, necessarily, from the immediacy of being. The absence is not an emptiness so much as a fullness of presence that is, while imaginable, not directly accessible. This pure presence is constantly suggested by each signifier's approach to its signified, but is not delivered. The supplement, as Derrida writes, is a promise of secure reference that escapes into other supplements;[11] it facilitates perception, for through it we compare and relate one thing to others, and yet sabotages, infinitely deflecting, ideal realisations. Hence, Derrida writes, "The sign is always a sign of the Fall".[12] Language closets a potential we can conceive but cannot encounter. The poet seeking absolute integrity finds, in Blanchot's words, "the abyss of the lost god, the infinite trace of absence, a moment to which Rilke comes closest perhaps in these three lines:

> O you, lost god! You, infinite trace!
> By dismembering you the hostile forces had to disperse you
> To make of us now hearers and a mouth of Nature."[13]

The notion of pure presence is, like Rilke's "lost god", a linguistic construction. We cannot know, in words, what it might entail, if it has meaning at all. It is not a state we can recall, nor one we can be sure is waiting to be discovered. Derrida says, "The sign is always a sign of the Fall", but he is careful to qualify the statement by insisting that the fall from full presence may have *always* already occurred. The gap between being and language, the gap that allows a sign to be a sign, and the gap that implies, without delivering, the possibility of a greater presence, is a condition, Derrida tells us, of textuality. It is a condition, we might conclude, of our particular kind of consciousness. "[I]t is perhaps given to us to 'live' each of the events that is ours", writes Blanchot,

> by way of a double relation. We live it one time as something we comprehend, grasp, bear, and master (even if we do so painfully and with difficulty) by relating it to some good or to some value, that is to say, finally, by relating it to Unity; we live it another time as something that escapes all employ and all end, and more, as that which escapes our very capacity to undergo it, but whose trial we cannot escape.[14]

We entertain beliefs and hopes amid a trial that nothing solves. We expend effort to sustain favoured impressions or to justify their alteration, and yet these impressions are formed and expressed through a medium that renders them incessantly questionable. Beside the teasing, distant promise of the perfect representation is the constant, invasive threat of imprecision and irrelevance.

This analysis of language is complicated by the observation that to be translated into words, being must first be perceived as something to which words can be applied. To be recognised as experiences, our feelings, actions, and ideas need *already* to have been partly signed. The sheer noise of each instant of being, of life itself, is delivered to consciousness via the filter of biological, cultural, and personal biases. These perceptual leanings need not all involve language directly, yet language cannot be ignored as a significant, contributing force. Relations between language and experience begin, then, prior to interpretative acts. Where, we might ask, does language end and experience start? There is no simple answer to this question. Yet, the pervasiveness of language does not remove experience from the equation. There are still feelings, events, and ideas that individuals do not find readily communicable. Immediacy and intimacy can seem, still, to be compromised by words. The "double relation" by which we live is not described by considering language and experience separately (since they are not entirely separable), but can be described as the duality of the idealisations we pursue through language and of the continuous sprawl of events and feelings that language influences but cannot seem to contain. Through the latter, we catch glimpses of the "trial we cannot escape". The blanket of language, we learn, is not woven so closely as to keep comprehension safe from the arrival of uncertainty, regarding both ourselves and the language we use.

The fall from full presence, the "double relation" Blanchot refers to, need not be considered unfortunate. "[N]o fullness," Blanchot tells us, "no certainty, can ever speak".[15] *Uncertainty*, the presence of absence, is the condition by which new expression becomes possible. The statement is central to the argument taken here and will be returned to in various forms. For the moment, however, the question is still how language might facilitate such a boon. The offered answer is again Derridean, though the relevance of Derrida's work is perhaps not immediately obvious. *De*construction exposes indeterminacies; creativity, on the other hand, requires the *con*struction of significant meaning. The two would seem to be opposed. Stuart Sim suggests that, "Derrida rescues us from the determinism of structure only to land us in the abyss between signifier and signified".[16] How, Sim asks, is a collapse into "a babble of incommensurable discourses" to be prevented?[17] Richard Kearney is equally suspicious: "If deconstruction prevents us from asserting or stating or identifying anything, then surely one ends up, not with 'difference', but with indifference, where nothing is anything, and everything is everything else?"[18]

Derrida works to expose, beneath the apparent rationality of existing texts, a language that cannot possibly deliver absolute meaning. He introduces the word *"différance"*, etymologically divided between "differ", "differre" (meaning, in Latin, to scatter, or disperse) and "defer",[19] to emphasise his argument. It is an intentionally confused term, offered both as a necessarily inadequate summary of the sprawl within signification *and* as an admitted, as-if-visible part of that sprawl, not, accordingly, as an easily determinable concept. Kevin Hart refers to *différance* as "that groundless condition of possibility and impossibility".[20] For Derrida, it is the "gift of the remain(s)";[21] elsewhere, Derrida refers directly to *différance* as "the possibility of conceptuality".[22] Why are these terms, gift and possibility, appropriate? The descriptions highlight a concern in Derrida's work not simply for taking texts apart, but for putting them together.[23] Famously, Derrida espouses "the joyous affirmation of the play of the world and of the innocence of becoming, the affirmation of a world of signs without fault, without truth, and without origin which is offered to an active interpretation".[24] The fall from full presence, the comment implies, is the chance for ongoing involvement in perceptual and conceptual renewal. We affirm our own participation in the world in which we find ourselves by taking the opportunity language offers for forging more and other interpretations.

Deconstruction, as Derrida offers it, decentres, fissuring and dislocating an expected rationality. It also insists, however, on a potential for more and other meaning. The boundaries of reason are unforgivingly deregulated but they are not obliterated: the urge for intelligibility is not denied. We cannot resist a transcendental reading absolutely, Derrida tells us, for this would "purely and simply destroy the trace of the text".[25] The "play of the world" is offered in opposition to the authority of convention, yet Derrida refuses to choose one or the other. He writes:

> But is not the desire for a center, as a function of play itself, the indestructible itself? And in the repetition or return of play, how could the phantom of the center not call to us? It is here that the hesitation between writing as decentring and writing as an affirmation of play is infinite. This hesitation is part of play and links it to death.[26]

The desire for a centre (death) and the desire for the breaking of centredness (play) turn out to be symbiotic. The hesitation that links them delivers the request and opportunity for interpretative involvement. We do not find *the* centre – "the entire history of the concept of structure," Derrida writes, "must be thought of as a series of substitutions of center for center"[27] – yet nor is there no centre. To create, or simply to perceive, is to insert pauses and summations into the infinite play of signification and to produce "decidables" even though already disseminated and, accordingly, *un*decidable. We relate each experience "to Unity", in Blanchot's terms (quoted above), even as each experience "escapes all employ and all end". Deconstruction need not be interpreted as celebrating dissemination *over* truth, or fragmentation *over* coherence (to this list V. Leitch adds "playfulness and hysteria over care and rationality"[28]), but as describing the presence of the former amid impressions of the latter. We work with both. The threat of greater fragmentation arrives with the teasing promise that there is also a potential for greater coherency. The force of *différance* lies in the notion that neither the threat nor the tease can be resolved. Even amid the most over-powering of centres there are opportunities for other interpretative *and thus expressive* possibilities. There is no room for simply any response at all, for the machine of language and the world that informs it must still be negotiated. Yet there is no external authority by which one might judge, incontestably, what can and cannot be attempted.

For Sim, Derrida

sounds like someone on the very threshold of the millennium, but, frustratingly for him, not quite able to break through. All he can do is to 'designate the crevice through which the unnameable glimmer beyond the closure can be glimpsed'.[29]

There is no need to assume that Derrida wants to "break through" anything. To arrive at "the unnameable glimmer" would be to lose the impetus for active interpretation, surely an undesirable result for one who celebrates the "gift of the remain(s)". If there is a threshold, it is one to approach and to draw influence from, and not one to defeat and leave behind. What is relished is not the thought of naming the unnameable glimmer but the promise and uncertainty of the new millennium that is (always) about to arrive. At such a threshold, language reveals what Hart describes as "its uncanny ability to produce *other* meanings at unpredictable times".[30] It reveals the chance to renew the range and effect of our expressions. The source of uncertainty is in the process undepleted, and expression, ideally, is reinvigorated. Language, for Derrida, is a carrier of both vision *and* indeterminacy, of coherency *and* play. The "and" is irreducible. Nietzsche, comparably, and informing Derrida, describes a "Dionysiac flood tide" that can always break through the circular ripples of Apollonian vision, disordering contemplation and illumination.[31] Apollo, the god of light and discernment, is a small vessel in stormy and unmeasured seas, floating in the "*superfluity of life* out of which the dionysian condition must again proceed".[32] Vision and expression are admitted and repeatedly re-admitted amid endless opportunities for constructing yet more and other *intelligible* illusions, none of which can boast immunity to revision. We are interpretatively alive, both writers insist, at the threshold between sense and uncertainty. Michael Serres, a writer also engaged by issues of non-finality and conceptual renewal, refers to a "touch of irrationality … a stroke of luck which gives us some breathing space, a loose fit in the machine which makes us alive".[33] For Serres, "non-completion does not mean ruinous residue or failure, but is the primary status of all things".[34] It is also, to borrow Serres's tone, the breath of vigour, an earth-caught auroral energy discharged again and again in ever-translatable images. Serres's *Genesis* offers an alternative metaphor: in Maria Assad's words,

> *Genèse* is Serres's attempt to unveil what has always been hidden in its starkness and nudity… Venus *and* the chaotic water, Venus *in* the ocean, the ocean clinging to Venus, chaos at the core of order and order within chaos. … She is Venus to whom viscidly cling the waters as she emerges and merges, in a thousand births, in multiple birthings, possibilities, and disappearances. She is equally the turbulent abyss that harbors limitless multiples and from which boils up, now and then, the exquisite form of one of those possibilities. She is the beautiful manifestation of order that is in chaos and chaos that is beautiful in its innumerable possibilities of phenomenal manifestations.[35]

To engage in creativity is to amplify the centre-play, Apollo-Dionysus, order-chaos simultaneity. The instabilities creators invite need not be extreme. In practice, innumerable standards and assumptions regarding language use are embraced without question. A poet integrated into a particular culture, fluent in a particular language, and practised in the conventions of his or her field, will not revise all or even most of the "centres" he or she refers to. Yet a threshold where perception ceases its subservience to already available conclusions, where meaning and representation are made to some extent insecure, will be somewhere arrived at. Subservience alone denies active (and creative) interpretation. The point to emphasise is that such a threshold is always available: language dictates that where there is coherency, or a potential for coherency, there will also be indeterminacy. What creators might do with the instabilities they admit, how particular decisions are facilitated in the midst of indeterminacy, and why such decision-making is pursued, are questions to be examined.

Interlude: Language

Language can guarantee nothing. A poem, as it appears on the page, is not the poem that is received, but the point at which indeterminacies are unleashed into acts of interpretation. The relay of indeterminacy can erupt into a strong sense of presence, and yet absence can never be far away. Meaning is fragile. The conventions that facilitate its construction cannot wholly hide the uncertainty.

Communiqué

Atomic ink (that says "Communiqué   Atomic ink (that says…)",
and then adds ", red in the poem's front window",
though the red fades), red in the poem's front window,

fading through plate glass and becoming
particles in atomic blue (the atomic ink, dispersing),
says (the ink says, as it rises),

the mind is that blue sky, collecting red (also
          , purple, splinters of r e , whatever
the poet fancies: indigo, rose…)

and at nightfall, what isn't lost in the starless ▮
recondenses: an image of a poem, called
(something like) "**Communiqué**"

Creative Redemption

The term "creative redemption" is offered here to describe a poet's response, and that of creators generally, to the uncertainties encountered in the act of creating new work. With Derrida still in mind, the idea of redemption may seem immediately contradictory. Derrida states that "The sign is always a sign of the Fall", and the claim has been that the uncertainties in language are unable to be resolved. The "Fall", further, has been portrayed as fortunate, yielding ongoing creative potential. What, then, is to be redeemed? Creative redemption refers not to the restoration of "pure presence", for absence is never defeated. It refers, rather, to a poet's arrival at a rewarding substitution. Blanchot describes the presence of absence by comparing it to a corpse. Extending the metaphor, it might be said that a poet responds to this absence not by bringing the corpse to life, but by writing an elegy for what has been lost. Following the writing of the elegy, the corpse will still be both with and not with the poet and the poem's readers, but the quality of their relations to the corpse will have changed. Ideally, the change revolves around the belief that a reflection of the fullness of presence, an emotional proof of its once-actual proximity, has been produced. The elegy then consoles, as a substitution for what it cannot become, and celebrates, at the same time, its own vitality, demonstrated through the vigour with which it aspires to compensate for the loss of life. The more convincing the elegy seems to be, the more able the poet and the poem's readers become with regard to their capacities to experience some sense of gain or reclamation. For the poet, this is the experience of creative redemption. Uncertainty may not be able to be eradicated (death is never cured), but a capacity for meaningful expression can still be affirmed, and affirmed with an intensity heightened by the proximity of death. But what counts, for a poet, as a substitution? Are all approaches to the fullness of presence equal?

In creativity, personalised use of an existing language coincides with a depersonalisation of specific sensibilities. Experiences that seem internal and subjective are translated into something external and publishable within a medium that is consequently extended. A work is constructed that is at once of and outside its maker. The resulting creation need not be revolutionary. The degree or conspicuousness of a creator's originality need not define his or her creativity. A sense of authorship is necessary, yet the process of finding expression for subjective impressions may yield only slight departures from convention and still seem significant to the creator concerned. What matters, with regard to creative redemption, is that renewed meaning or feeling can seem to be arrived at despite and because of encountered uncertainties. The threat of absence, the threat of meaninglessness or irrelevance, can seem to be (temporarily and provisionally) defeated. In poetry, and equivalently in other fields, the resulting poem or poetic effect becomes, for its author, satisfying and persuasive. Rather than mourning the presence of absence, the poem is seen to evidence that not all has been disabled. Not all potency, the poet is able to claim, has passed into the grave. The achievement is not absolute. The fullness of presence is that space, borrowing from Blanchot (writing, in turn, in response to Rilke),

> to which the poet doubtless has no access, where he can penetrate only to disappear, which he attains only when he is united with the intimacy of the breach that makes him a mouth unheard, just as it makes him who hears into the weight of silence.[36]

A poet would enter such a space, the comment implies, only by becoming the corpse itself. The substitution is the ambition to produce a work that is strong enough, or novel enough, to disguise, for a time, the absence that will not dissolve. To renew poetic expression, to deliver, however minimally, an effect or meaning not previously known, is to indeed imply that a gap has been filled, namely the gap the new work occupies. The sense of redemption can be rewarding, though it does not reduce the scope for more and other poems: absence retains its presence and the substitution can be repeated indefinitely.

It is fair to ask how a creator can know when or if a redeeming work has been produced. When, returning to Serres's metaphor, can Venus be said to be sufficiently clear of the water, of which she is in any case a part? Predictably, there can be no sure answer. Poets' conceptions of what is satisfying in their own poetry will be informed by numerous comparisons with other poems. They will also be informed by personal and social influences outside the field of poetry. Each bias will be unique, but will also be joined to the network of meanings, historical, physical, and social, that describe the practices and cultures of which the poets are a part. We narrate our existence, Alasdair MacIntyre reminds us, using story lines that are neither told entirely for us nor entirely by us.[37] In the poststructural terms of Jean-François Lyotard, "we have always already been told something, and we have always already been spoken".[38] We are not free to tell simply any story at all. We are held by the viscosities of our time. Poets, if they are to perceive themselves *as* poets, will write themselves into stories about poetry. Before there can be participation in meaningful poetic exchange, sufficient conceptual reference points need to be developed regarding what poetry is and why it tends to be written. The writing of poetry, in other words, is in part contractual. In consequence, the choices arresting play and multiplicity (and releasing it into other regions) may *seem* like choices and not random fluctuations; impressions of consistency and of valid reasoning become attainable.

Creative redemption is experienced in relation to the historical, social, and conceptual conditions that allow work on a particular poem to seem, to the poet concerned, both possible and worthwhile. The various kinds of contracts these conditions help to shape are the topics of sections II and III (to follow). It needs to be emphasised, however, that the presence of such contracts, and of the story line to which they contribute, locates but does not itself answer the question of how a poet is to recognise a moment of creative redemption. Even within the most detailed of story lines, there can be no point of reference by which a creation might be judged absolutely. Contracts can always be to some extent renegotiated and there are consequently no firm means of assessing individual poems. A sonnet that seems to fail to meet the standard set by previous sonnets may be seen, in other eyes, to set a new standard for the sonnets yet to be written. A creator can ultimately rely only on his or her own (informed) opinion. Hence, an extreme personalisation of an existing language, a degree of originality, in other words, that threatens or denies public access to a work, may still seem legitimate to its author. There are examples of creators, Emily Dickinson is one, Gerard Manley Hopkins is another, who continued to create while their works remained largely unseen or misunderstood, or were forcefully rejected. These creators' capacities to carry on communicating to an absent audience highlights a quality of the contracts with which they were involved. Poets participate in a community of ideas. Imagining the presence of a work within such a community may be a poet's prime means of assessing its impact. The important illusion here is that the community exists "out there": a poet's individual influence is to be injected into (an internalised impression of) something outside him- or herself. The translation converts the poet's bias into an event within a somewhat impersonal, textual reality. The poem is to become, for its author, at once intimate and independent. To work *within* a poetic community is to travel out, conceptually, to a poetic location where the poem just written will hopefully survive in its own right. Poets conceive of themselves as writers of poetry perhaps by convincing themselves that their poems have in this way "arrived".

But can a creation be part of a larger, impersonal network of meaning if no one else understands it? A maverick creator might claim that it can. Able to perceive, in his or her work, value that others fail to see, and able to believe the work has a place in the community of ideas to which it is offered, such a creator may find the strength to imagine that somewhere, or somewhen, there is an audience able to share his or her view. Many creators look for more tangible encouragement. Even with such encouragement, however, maverick-style self-assessment cannot be altogether avoided. Creative redemption is achieved subjectively and without assurances. The bias, the rigour, the desires, and the daring with which particular creators explore and respond to their chosen fields and mediums will vary with the experiences, capabilities, and psychology of each individual, and with the circumstances of each creative act. Redemptive sensations are dependent on a particular state of being. It is entirely possible that the effects would be, in certain situations, impermanent, even though the work referred to remained unchanged.

Creators have at various times attempted to bypass or at least to minimise the contractual framing of creativity. In so-called automatic writing (pursued by various writers from the 1920s onwards), the intent, as Blanchot explains, was to "put the hand that writes in contact with something original".[39] Via the rapid recording of what were termed "free" associations, direct access was to be gained to uncensored, uncompromised expression. A more recent and no less frustrated attempt to escape contractuality is illustrated by the blurred boundaries and "ungoverned" text of what has become known as Language Poetry. At first glance, this poetry seems to demand that internal, subjective play is a sufficient beginning *and end* for a legitimate creation. Much of Lyn Hejinian's poetry, for instance, performs a music of associations that seems never to have been intended to mimic the species of authority relied on in the poetic canon. "Some see loud apples falling", Hejinian writes,

> with less decision than likeness
> It catches the night light
> White line
> And what of the listener?
> That light is intellectually collapsing
> There are such individual emotions
> > that anyone knows oneself unprepared
> > with half-hoping adjustment but unsolved
> > cave
> Heat fills the ocean with
> > bed – but incompletely and brightly
> > at the same time it's never entirely closed [40]

Words, here, merge into effects that lose reason to a larger picture of a sprawling mind, a mind before being ordered by conventional logic. Yet logic prevails. Hejinian's achievement has been to transform personal associations into a publicly available (and somewhat limited) signifier: the work becomes a symbol of subjectivity itself. To redeem one's subjectivity by convincing oneself (and others) of its inherent worth is to intelligibly identify (an appropriately formalised) "subjectivity". In this case, it is a "subjectivity" associable with the somewhat political intent of exposing, by swerving from, a subservience to an expected rationality. The work, of course, by being interpretable as such, fails to escape this rationality. It is for Hejinian as it is for deconstruction: "We have", Derrida explains,

> no language – no syntax and no lexicon – which is foreign to this history [of metaphysics]; we can pronounce not a single destructive proposition which has not already had to slip into the form, the logic, and the implicit postulations of precisely what it seeks to contest.[41]

We cannot choose to not relate our words and deeds to the words and deeds around us. We cannot sanely escape into pure irrationality, though impressions of, or allusions to such freedom may be constructed. A creation is always, to some extent, a conventional argument, claiming at the very least that it is itself a legitimate thing for a creator to produce. Terry Eagleton, interpreting Theodor Adorno, offers that art

> appears as the process by which rationality criticizes itself without being able to overcome itself. ...The more the work of art seeks to liberate itself from external determinations, the more it becomes subject to self-positing principles of organization... [A]rt holds out against domination in its respect for the sensuous particular, but reveals itself again and again as an ideological ally of such oppression.[42]

Creative redemption consoles amid this entrapment in our own uncertain reasoning. It is the celebration of that degree of freedom that allows us to move from one principle of organisation to another, and to glimpse, between the two, our own capacity for renewal. The sensuous particular is as-if approached, its representation being sharpened by the new substitution our creative powers deliver.

Interlude: Redemption

Thom Gunn claims to find material for poems by reaching into

unexplained areas of the mind, in which the air is too thickly primitive or too fine for us to live continually. From that reaching I bring back loot, and don't always know at first what that loot is.[43]

A loose association between two things, a vaguely identified emotion, a certain sound or silence… these are a few examples of the loot Gunn refers to. Faced with the uncertainty in such material, a poet's challenge is to construct significant meaning, or a significant and independent experience, in which others may participate. Allow, for example, an association between the heart and a stringed instrument. What can be done with such a dream, with what is essentially an error? What persuasion can be created to prevent it from being dismissed as a meaningless aberration?

Song

love presses

like a lute
on the rib cage,

strung inside the heart.

Contractuality – an Overview

Creativity is a response, often a sought response, to uncertainty. It is a response kept alive by the impossibility of arriving at absolute certainty and by, at once, the possibility of producing a significant (and redemptive) surrogate. For poets, linguistic indeterminacies yield endless opportunities for creative expression. They are not the only uncertainties poets encounter, nor are they conducive to poetic creativity in isolation. The contracts, or story lines, poets embrace, the conditions they accept and negotiate in order to perceive themselves as poets, lend direction. They introduce, also, further sources of absence and ambiguity – there are no transcendental story lines. The nature of poetic contracts and the uncertainties that are invited by them are examined in detail in the chapters that follow. The relations between language, experience, and poetic expression, as implied by these contracts, remain the central point of focus. In section II, attention is given to the technical contracts poets embrace. Creative redemption, it is argued, is experienced relative, in part, to a poet's knowledge and perceptions of poetic forms and techniques. By negotiating a particular technical contract, by deciding to write, for example, a Shakespearean sonnet, a limerick, or a Language poem, a poet can set a challenge that both channels and amplifies his or her creative efforts. Ambitions, doubts, rewards, and disappointments can all be intensified. Since contracts can always be revised, a chosen poetic form can also become a site for experimentation. Uncertainty can be drawn from the question of how much and what kind of divergence from convention might be satisfying in a poem, and from the risk that this divergence might yield a contract the poet concerned cannot fulfil. The need for redemption may seem, in such contexts, all the more urgent.

In section III, attention is given to what are termed the "aesthetic" contracts of poetry and to the multiple psychological pressures and motivations that contribute to experiences of creative pleasure. When is creativity perceivable as worthwhile or appealing? What qualities in a poem, or in the act of writing, facilitate such appeal? Which needs and ideals might spur and sustain a poet's efforts? In considering these questions, the pleasure and pain a creator experiences while creating, and his or her organisations of these feelings (into, for example, hope and endurance), is given relation to expectations within the field. The pressure issuing from the need for creators to diverge in their work from the sources of authority they are to simultaneously consult, by the need, in other words, to produce something recognisably poetic but also recognisably individual, is especially noted. This tension accents the notion that what is to be created is the very work that is absent from the field as it stands. The task of the modern poet, it declares, is to reveal what is missing in poetic expression; it is to renew and modernise our representations of being, and, by implication (though forever illusively), to draw poetic expression closer to being itself. The impact of a poet's personal needs and anxieties on this and the other aesthetic contracts he or she negotiates is also discussed. Creative redemption, it is argued, is experienced not simply with the arrival of an end product, but through satisfying involvement in what can be unforgiving and indeterminate processes and ideals. A poet cannot know precisely what is needed to effect compelling, poetic expressions, and cannot be sure, in any particular instance, that either he or she or the medium has what it takes to produce the desired poem. Amid such uncertainty, the idea and/or experience of redemption can carry considerable psychological weight.

Technical and aesthetic contracts are pursued, in creativity, in conjunction with efforts to express or make sense of subjective associations. It need not be clear which comes first – curiosity regarding a technique, or a desire for a certain quality of expression, may lead to, emerge with, and/or follow a particular thematic interest. A given creation is likely to involve realisations on all three levels. The urge to express internal, subjective impressions, and the compromises necessitated by the translation of these impressions into poetry, are considered in section I. Here, emphasis is given to the broad context for creative work, namely the formation, from internal associations, of publishable expression. Direct transcriptions of subjective impressions are intrinsically impossible. We create amid what Christopher Norris describes, deconstructively, as "the 'abysmal' slippages and detours of all understanding".[44] Persuasion, section I argues, becomes the work of the poet.

In practice, the thematic, technical, and aesthetic elements of poetic creativity each inform the other. The interactions are complex. Poetic forms and ideals become part of what allows close attention to be given to particular thoughts and experiences, and may themselves contribute to what those experiences are perceived to be. There is no division in this process to match that given in the chapters of this book. The separation is a mere convenience.

Intermission: Uncertainty

The gap between language and experience, the presence of absence, does not alter the fact that we are dependent on the impressions of order language nonetheless allows. The ridge between knowing and not knowing is an invitation for involvement.

hieroglyphic

crawling into his ears, the scratchings
of his pen gnaw on the sinews
to his heart;

the loudest of words
spill back into his field of vision
and he strains to hear

what was audible, or so he dreams,
before the pen
was raised;

hieroglyphs
scatter from the vowels he utters,
and his view,

filtered by their lines, shows only glimmers
of its promise; but he writes,
sifting for what remains.

Bartering with a young child

Words stumble on him, hammering for a place of entry.
Some collapse on his mind's floor and idle,
waiting for contact. A few
fall onto his rough tongue, and he rolls them
past lips enamoured only of textures.

Language in me stoops to hold him;
its slip resounds. I tell him I wasn't born this way.
I tell him there's forgetfulness, but he lends his hand,
and on the fringe of silence, ears pressed to our passing,
we walk as if time can't end.

Short legs break small time into fields
and we feed the ducks on what tears
from my years of reason. Near the river-reeds,
there are flowers no-one's planted, and we carry blooms
back from the foreshore.

And it's true: the colour fades, the sap bleeds:
at fence lines, I'm loosened from their fragrance;
at the house, the child uncurls his fingers – he's hurling vowels
back the way we came, and words
fill the hollows of my skull. The world evicts us.

Yet at nightfall, before he sleeps, this child finds me,
pulls me into his arms, and his touch,
dark-bright and wordless, tells me
in our palms there are wild seeds, and in the distance,
the prospering of unwritten hours.

Gap:

to inhabit a wasteland,
the noise inside the silence,

nerve cells not broken
by the birth of voice, a womb

still bleeding what
syntax doesn't notice…

in an underland
in the shadows of the eye.

Language

like chewing
with someone else's saliva.

rumours of first-hand accounts
even of pterosaurs.

Making Our Minds Up

Never enough pieces to build the drawbridge.

All care, and still the acoustics
tangle in the echoes of "mum and dad".

Tom says Juanita's always in his mind
playing poker with his house of cards.

Ria forgets to take her torch
when she leaves from Mark's place
and doesn't get home.
She's in the high street,
hoping he'll come and get her.

Stella runs out of glue...

There's a made-up mind just waiting
on an empty table in the cafeteria.

Sebastian's three tips for cleaning cobwebs
off the insides of cathedral domes
don't help at all.

The inventory: one shelf, a hammer, 403 screws;
the shelf's pre-drilled – none of the screws fit.

"The mind," says the body,
"never knew what it was doing:
leave the pieces on the floor
and walk away".

Mick gave Sally
what his dad gave him
when things didn't fit together.
He wants to know if she's using it
and can he have it back.

Moira waits for a commission.

Bruce
bakes a six-layered,
kirsch gâteau;
everyone's impressed.

…And Zali's wine! (days later, Liam's
stashed bottle is over the hill, and no one cares).

Sure

sand, still stony with belief, the mason's promise
pressed over crumbling grains
to hide the erosion.

relativity

all his thought
in a night sky:
a toy constellation;

tendons stretching back
to the vocal cords
melt, leaving

eyes in midnight:
day still arrives
but with no umbilical

Section I: Translation

The Treachery of Language

Words and experiences fail to fit neatly together. There are no sure ways of describing events and feelings without also re-casting them. What is written will be both more and less than was sensed or imagined. All of language becomes involved, with all of its contrivances, and with all of its attachments to more and other language. Signification, Blanchot observes, bears "a strange impersonal light".[45] "In speech", he writes, "what dies is what gives life to speech; speech is the life of that death, it is 'the life that endures death and maintains itself in it'".[46] To use specifically poetic language is to yield and to inhabit a death of a particular kind. Poems are not sincere translations of particular encounters but progressions from those encounters to communicable poetic effects. This is not to suggest that sincerity is necessarily abandoned but that it becomes (perhaps awkwardly) divided: a poet's commitment is to the subjects he or she entertains *and* to poetry. While the impressions a poet desires to translate may die for the sake of the poem, they need not decay – almost paradoxically, the life of the poem holds them from this fate. Why inflict the death at all?

The treachery of language is unavoidable. Terry Eagleton details the dilemma: "How can the mind", he writes,

> not betray the object in the very act of possessing it, struggling to register its density and recalcitrance at just the point it impoverishes it to some pallid universal? It would seem that the crude linguistic instruments with which we lift a thing towards us, preserving as much as possible of its unique quality, simply succeed in pushing it further away. In order to do justice to the qualitative moments of the thing, thought must thicken its own texture, grow gnarled and close-grained; but in doing so it becomes a kind of object in its own right, sheering off from the phenomenon it hoped to encircle. As Theodor Adorno remarks: 'the consistency of its performance, the density of its texture, helps the thought to miss the mark'.[47]

Even the pallid universal is not what it seems, its incessant allusion to more and other signs leaving little but the hope (founded on convention) that its reference will be effective. "Gnarled and close-grained thought", like a Derridean "centre", keeps us from drowning in too much margin. Distortive, the gnarling nonetheless facilitates intelligible exchange. It is for these reasons that "The treachery of language," as Alex Skovron writes in the poem "Quadrilateral", "leads us back / like shadows to a torch".[48] A poet's struggle lies in finding a way to "miss the mark" persuasively. Via a language that cannot "hit the mark", he or she is to construct, nonetheless, an impression that it has. A poem's "sheering off" from the phenomena that inspire it, and its emergence as an "object in its own right" (or more often, an *event*), is a result of this process. Distortion, suppression, and elaboration of selected (and some unselected) materials necessarily takes place.

Blanchot, too, emphasises the inevitability of the betrayal, insisting that it is only by defending against that which inspires that anything can be produced. It is as if, he states, one couldn't write except – since one must write – by resisting the pure need to write, by avoiding the approach of what is to be written, that word without beginning or end which we cannot express except by silencing it. This is the magic torment which is linked to the call of inspiration. One necessarily betrays it: and not because books are only the degraded echo of a sublime word, but because one only writes them by silencing what inspires them, by failing the movement they claim to recall, by interrupting 'the murmur'.[49]

Blanchot assumes, romantically, a depth and purity of inspiration that not all poets will or need necessarily recognise. The comment's exuberance, however, does not destroy its relevance. The act of betrayal, Blanchot confirms, the silencing or muffling of the continuity of our experiences (where the gap between language and experience interrupts the murmur of being, rendering it both present and absent), is also the process by which poems are written. Is the act one of exploitation? Is experience lost to the glory of what is written? Might an elegy, for example, be considered less an honest response to loss than an attempt to capitalise on a strong emotion – why is the poem written if not to impress? In answer: a lack of compassion or of morality need not be assumed. Elegists can indeed be expected to strive to produce the best poems they can with the materials that are available. It cannot be concluded that they will not also attempt an honest response to an experience of loss, but this response will be in part withheld, or as Blanchot writes, resisted. More so than for everyday conversation, a poem, since it is produced as a work of art as well as a means of communication, will diverge from that which inspires it. Yet meaningful exchange can take place. What is written can be an expression of events and feelings that others may relate to in ways not facilitated by everyday language. That which allows exploitation in poetry allows, also, the effects for which poetry is pursued and for which it is celebrated.

Treachery has its advantages. As W.S. Graham describes, language is "obstacle and vehicle at the same time".[50] This is to say, as has been argued in the introduction, that there is, in language, both uncertainty and the opportunity for redemption, both absence, in other words, and the chance to construct a surrogate for that absence. With regard to the relations between uncertainty and redemption in poetic creativity, the treachery of language has further significance. For a poet, it is as an obstacle that language can be most enabling. Referring to interpretations of texts, Derrida offers that the absence of unequivocal, translatable identities "starts reading and writing and translation moving again. The unreadable is not the opposite of the readable but rather the ridge {arête} that also gives it momentum, movement, sets it in motion".[51] Unreadability, uncontainable and unlocatable, Derrida adds, "gives, presents, permits, yields something to be read".[52] This is the "gift of the remain(s)"[53] already referred to. For a writer, the absence of any means for direct representation can give momentum to creative involvement; undecidability gives, presents, permits, yields something to be created. "We find ourselves", Hart explains,

> losing the origin that once attracted us to a work, and being approached by an irruption in immanence, not a transcendence but an infinite dispersal of indeterminate being. As if trapped, we yield to the fascination this irruption exerts in language, giving ourselves over to the allure of the imaginary.[54]

We ask language to furnish us with secure references and it presents us with infinitely many possible associations. For a poet, these possibilities (substitutes for an *im*possibility) are the opportunity to find what it was not known could be said. Deconstruction tells us that nothing that is found can bear any special legitimacy. Amid this play of signification, the task is to redeem, by constructing belief, the sense that this indeterminacy can be contained. The bliss of convention is that it offers both a frame *and* looseness. It is not just that uncertainty in language inspires an urge for redemption, but that it can be encountered at a location (a point of departure) at which creative endeavours can begin. Partially liberated from impressions of certainty, but not immersed, either, in pure *un*certainty, the poet is able to give him- or herself over to "the allure of the imaginary".

Poets create by finding in the machine of language springs they did not know were loose, and can be incited to do so by the difficulties that machine introduces into their efforts to translate specific impressions. For Adrienne Rich, a poem

> engenders new sensations, new awareness in me as it progresses … instead of poems *about* experiences I am getting poems that *are* experiences, that contribute to my knowledge and my emotional life even while they reflect and assimilate it.[55]

The treachery of language is a means for exploration, offering the chance to assay associations and effects through which new impressions of significance, sought or unexpected, might emerge. Can we conclude, then, that poetic creativity is impeded if betrayal and indeterminacy are too strongly resisted? The answer is yes. The denial inflicted on a poem by a poet too attached to his or her sources of influence, a poet too immediately and insistently involved in the instigating events, can indeed be problematic and has been noted by a number of writers. It deserves some comment:

Perceptions of what has been and might yet be achieved poetically in a poem can be marred by a loss of concentration to the personal importance both of the subjects to be translated and of the poem itself. The allure of the imaginary can be dulled by a fixed and non-poetic commitment to personal meanings. It cannot be considered that a poet ever knows precisely where his or her poetic and non-poetic interests begin and end. Certain assumptions may be so deeply embedded in a poet's perception that their influence within a work remains hidden or unstated. To some extent this is inevitable. The consequences, though, can be severe and inevitability does not remove the need for vigilance. Stern warnings have been given by a number of poets. W.H. Auden insists that, "unless the poet sacrifices his feelings completely to the poem so that they are no longer his but the poem's, he fails".[56] T.S. Eliot calls for "a continual extinction of personality".[57] James Engell, summarising Keats and borrowing, accordingly, a Romantic turn of phrase, describes the clarity that can be gained when one "merges the self in the world" and loses "the sullied accidents and inevitable restrictions of the ego".[58] It is easy to imagine, here, a transcendent state of empathic selflessness where one must be in order to write good poetry. In reality, an eradication of personality (were it possible) could only deny the motivations and peculiarities that enable new poems to be written. Yet, if a poem is to seem to enter that community of poetic ideas that exists "outside" any individual poet, as the discipline of redemption requests (the discipline in which experiences that seem internal and subjective are translated into something external and publishable), then non-poetic attachments must seem, at some stage, to lose priority to a poetic contract. It need not be immediately obvious to an author how a work is not, or how it might become, independent. The aspirations that might drive the required endeavour are the concern of section III.

To admit and to utilise uncertainty is to invite a certain kind of exchange. There are risks, and conditions apply. These are the concerns of the chapter that follows.

Interlude: Never Hitting the Mark

Ted Hughes writes, "In a way, words are continually trying to displace our experience"; experiences themselves, he adds, "embed themselves in us quite a long way from the world of words".[59] If the experience is highly unusual, unlike anything previously reported, this distance might seem all the more marked. The struggle to find words to contain without compromising what has been witnessed, words that will not seem to invent their own meanings, might seem particularly acute.

(In 1960, US air force colonel, Joe Kittinger, leapt from a helium balloon, 30 000 metres above the ground; a tear in one of his gloves caused an injury to his hand. The footage is still occasionally aired.)

Blue Balloon

A man jumps from a helium balloon, thirty thousand metres
above the ground, with a parachute, and swallows memories
no-one else can apprehend. / The Earth's blue verges into black,
he's *in* the black, and there's no ripple in the suit he wears, so
is he falling? / The balloon slips at supersonic speeds into a
backdrop he can't hold: the sun boils in a night sky, and time
pours through him...

> *He wants it back, the four-minute free-fall, the sun*
> *blinding and the dark chewing into his bones.*
> *The blue sifts his remains.*

A pinprick in the left glove admits the hug of the sky's edge, and the
flesh swells and desiccates... / But heals. / And there's no scar. / He
searches for a tinge of dark in the lifeline of his left hand, and curls
his palm as if to keep it there. / It's a test of the abrasion...

> *Earth's greens bombard him. He likes*
> *this about them: the pigments seep deeper into his*
> *splintered cells, as if each leaf is inside him. He*
> *likes, too, the sense of organism, pounding through his*
> *heart, the infinite, picking at his fingers.*

Up

Footage of a man jumping from a helium balloon
at a height that has him falling through a black sky
in daytime, renders the man watching him,
forty years later (couch pulled up close to a
full-colour screen) slightly unsettled: mild terror
spreads across the room, shrinking it to its actual size.

    All morning, he's searching the sky for imprints
    from where the black's fingers keep their purchase
    on the husk of his own life, expecting airmen
    to appear from nowhere, or the remnants
    of the man's balloon, finally plunging. He fancies
    faint constellations – scratch marks across the blue.

He fetches his best saw. Says he wants/needs
a larger window, and he cuts. And the sky
edges into his living room… Night still arrives,
but he's pleased – the balloon event
teleports into his own renaissance: he doesn't move,
drifting in the night's stars; and come morning,

        the view astounds – his breath
        spills through his whole backyard.

Uncertainty

Poetry is not granted the poet as a truth and a certainty against which he could measure himself. He does not know whether he is a poet, but neither does he know what poetry is, or even whether it is. It depends on him, on his search. And this dependence does not make him master of what he seeks; rather, it makes him uncertain of himself and as if nonexistent. Every work, and each moment of the work, puts everything into question all over again; and thus he who must live only for the word has no way to live.[60]

Poets distort subjectively interpreted materials in their efforts to satisfy poetic contracts that are themselves negotiable. The negotiations are not definitely contained: there are no absolute boundaries that define what "poetic" may or may not mean. Examples of past poems abound, but perceptions of them vary, and none portray what poetry may yet become. Whether or not a poem is successful will be a question ambivalently answered: "it seems so to me" is the best conclusion its author can offer, and to this she or he might add, "at least, it seems so some of the time". Blanchot, the author of the quotation given above, offers these uncertainties in their extreme. A poet, the comment implies, is not primarily insightful or skilful, but sceptical, unsure, even, of what it can mean to create. The poet Blanchot depicts is one able to step back from *all* of the assumptions and contrivances that form poetic and larger communities. It is not suggested here that such acute suspicion is necessary in a poet, or even common, if it is, indeed, possible. Yet none of our assumptions and contrivances are ever beyond questioning. Blanchot intensifies uncertainties that are always at least imaginable and that filter through our defences to become sources of creative potential. In the previous chapter, it was suggested that uncertainty in language, in addition to driving a general urge for redemption, can spur specific creative explorations. Under what conditions can uncertainty function in this way?

A poet's play with indeterminacy need not be visible as such within the poem that is produced. In apparent contradiction to this statement, John Forbes' "Orange Sonnet" reads,

> oranges in my experience not yet ripe
> and eaten in our hands or on plates
> at more formal, unsticky consumptions
> they stain neglected fruitbowls rot
> a delicate green the New South Wales
> Railways believe them I dont impolite
> in trains where my head as yours needs
> patches of immediate bright colour
> the visual excitement now consisting
> of TV's off-white shirts and blood
> and only the rare festal occasions we
> get balloons like spring frocks and
> their contents one should write a poem
> about oranges, possibly long[61]

Traditional poetic logic is not forgotten here but nor is it wholly confirmed. Fleeting and equivocal impressions are privileged at the expense of conventional subjects. Readers may find the poem humorous, they may see in it a reflection of a familiar state of mind, yet there is a sense in which the poem remains unintelligible. Why invite such ambiguity? The poem, importantly, like all poems, was not written in isolation. Forbes' works are distinctively his own, and yet are also expressions of his cultural (and poststructural) surroundings. The notion that sprawling and entangled associations are as much a part of perception as neatly ordered explications was readily available to Forbes, from multiple poetic and philosophical sources. Does the poem conform, then, to a bias of its time? In part it does. A poet, Hart argues, risks "new feelings and new meanings" by "taking the known in tandem with the unknown".[62] Hart names John Ashbery, René Char, Roberto Juarroz and Tomas Transtromer, but the comment is more broadly applicable. It describes the gamble that can only be altogether avoided through a denial of creativity. The "known" is that through which the "unknown" can begin to be perceived, and in relation to which the risks creativity necessarily entails can be devised and taken. Uncertainty is not employable as a force in its own right. Nothing can be achieved if what Blanchot terms "the intimacy of the risk", the risk, that is, that we will be "introduced, utterly without reserve, into a place where nothing retains us at all", is not glimpsed from *within reason*.[63] Dionysus can only contribute to creativity if there is also Apollo; indeterminacy can wield no influence if there is not also vision. If "Orange Sonnet" carries evidence of the uncertainties its author responded to, then this evidence lies not in the poem's overt ambiguities, but in the risks it takes relative to what was, for Forbes, already familiar.

To take the known in tandem with the unknown is to find sufficient uncertainty to engage and challenge without overwhelming one's will to respond. It is to identify a suitable degree of risk, though what this degree is will depend on the poem and poet concerned. The broken words, crippled syntax, and distorted punctuation used by e.e. cummings provide an obvious example of creative daring, but small details within largely conventional poems can also offer opportunities for creativity. How is it sensible, though, to speak of finding "sufficient" uncertainty when Blanchot and Derrida have already told us that there is an infinite supply? In answer, it is a matter not of *finding* uncertainty so much as of allowing some fraction of it to be unveiled. "Reason supervises us, the critical intellect restrains us, we speak according to customs and conventions", Blanchot writes.[64] There is, returning to Derrida, a "phantom of the centre", even amid "a world of signs without fault, without truth, and without origin".[65] To create is to find, first, an opening in the existing codes of reason, a foothold in the climb up onto the ridge of indeterminacy. It is to disrupt, fortuitously or by intent, elements of the relations that form familiar meanings, allowing the ordinary and the familiar, as Hart writes, quoting Blanchot, to "appear as 'an anonymous, distracted, deferred, and dispersed way of being in relation', and not, as we expect, comforting, known, and readily mastered".[66] Disruption is always theoretically possible; centres can be infinitely re-centred. Yet there is much at stake. "To write", Hart tells us, "is to risk losing one's relation to meaning and the world or, equally, to risk finding oneself in relation with what has no meaning and no world".[67] Uncertainty is to be both valued and feared.

Poets invite uncertainty into contexts that promise some degree of containment. They invite them, further, only with the promise of some reward. By definition, a creator is one who approaches uncertainty with the aim, or the dream, of constructing new relevance or interest. The task is to draw unknowns to where attention can be given to them *and then to resolve them* as far as possible, despite the risk this entails, the risk, namely, that the resulting work will yield only small, or no, significance. Uncertainty is entertained, dangerously, for the opportunity to test the force (*against* uncertainty) of particular actions and ideas. Poetic revelations, Wallace Stevens writes, "are not the revelations of belief, but the precious portents of our own powers".[68] The comment can be appropriated to emphasise the chance poets have, in creativity, to evidence their influence both over the knowledge they possess *and* over the "as yet unnameable", "formless" and "terrifying" (as Derrida terms it).[69] Again, the threat effected by a poet's willingness to invite uncertainty into his or her work need not be large. The "as yet unnameable" (what Blanchot refers to as "the menacing proximity of a vague and vacant outside, a neutral existence, nil and limitless"[70]) is never tackled outside the frame of convention, and the frame itself may leave only the slightest of openings through which the formless and the terrifying can be glimpsed. A sense of power remains on offer. The promise of a poem's realisation waits for the actual poem to be written and for the adequacy of the available means, both personal and poetic, to be perceived. This is always the case, and the allure in finding and responding to the uncertainties involved is surely part of what it means to create. Such allure is implied by William Stafford's assertion that what he looks for, as he writes, is "the suspenseful emergence of satisfying realizations".[71] Brendan Kennelly, similarly, identifies the chance to resolve unknowns as a motivation for his work. Uncertainties, Kennelly writes, "demand to be uttered in all their challenging, disruptive force".[72] For Robert Penn Warren, too, poems begin often as a response to materials that induce discomfort, "especially", Warren writes, "if you are uncomfortable because you don't quite understand all that it means".[73] There is reward, the examples reiterate, in redeeming the sense of order uncertainty threatens. Redemption, of course, is never assured.

The quest for redemption is noted, too, by Harold Bloom. Bloom, however, goes on to emphasise that the quest has no end. The creative mind, Bloom observes (in his reading of Stevens), "is never-resting because it knows its own status as fiction, and in knowing that, it knows delight, as untruth and as poetry"; "it knows", Bloom adds, "the heat of the unfinished and of the unfinishable".[74] Here, Bloom places uncertainty at the core of a poet's experiences. In the absence of assurance and completion, delight can be found in the energy and revelation induced by the pursuit of appealing fictions, fictions that redeem expression from the threat of doubt and undecidability *impermanently* and thus redeliver the opportunity to create. In the heat of the unfinishable, creative redemption is experienced with each fiction's delightful effect, an effect that is to pass into other fictions. "Poetry does not reveal the meaning of being through the genius of a poet," Hart tells us, "but holds being and meaning together for a while in an intense and unequal relationship".[75] The comment supports Bloom's claim. In a redeeming poem, both writers imply, the relationship between being and meaning is contingent and always already a part of a larger potential for yet more and other meaning. The redemption, to return to an earlier metaphor, is elegiac. It celebrates "the precious portents of our own powers", but can only console with regard to the absence language inflicts. A poem is a surrogate and not certainty itself. This, too, is a condition under which uncertainty is employed.

Hart continues the argument. "Poets begin romantically," he writes,

> in quest of the meaning of being, and in that moment accept or evade what forces itself upon them: that being and meaning fail to co-incide. In this way a poet may try to write just one poem, the one that seems to call both day and night, only to write hundreds of poems over a lifetime. A poem calls with the force of necessity, yet it gets written and rewritten as the necessarily accidental.[76]

The romanticism Hart refers to resides in the notion that behind the threat of indeterminacy lies a more profound potential, the potential for an expression in which being and meaning do finally find each other. It is as if "clouds of inauthenticity", Ann Smock surmises, keep a poem "like a flower just on the sheer verge of blooming".[77] The romantic believes the bloom will arrive and that the presence of absence will dissolve. Jahan Ramazani, quoting from the first poem of "Prologues to What Is Possible", tells us that Stevens

> feels himself drawn onward by a desirable end – an end that shatters the mirrors of appearance and rejoins him to the One 'at a point of central arrival, an instant moment.' Lured by a meaningless 'syllable' that nevertheless 'contained the meaning into which he wanted to enter,' the poet sails beyond the deferrals of language, attaining at last the completion of his life's meaning.[78]

The idea that there can be direct access to things as they essentially are (including ourselves) gains expression in Stevens' "Notes Towards a Supreme Fiction". There are occasions, the poem promises, when we can glimpse a subject of interest and

> ...catch from that

> Irrational moment its unreasoning,
> As when the sun comes rising, when the sea
> Clears deeply, when the moon hangs on the wall

> Of heaven-haven.[79]

Yet Stevens recognises that an awareness of such moments necessarily introduces influences that do not belong to them. In the same poem, the desire to depict the pure meaning of being is shown to be fraught with impossibility; expression, the poem argues, is never innocent. A woman is described as being able to glimpse her children *as they are*, but she cannot translate the experience: "And what she felt," Stevens writes, "fought off the barest phrase".[80] Another of Stevens' poems, "The Poems of Our Climate", claims,

> ...delight,
> Since the imperfect is so hot in us,
> Lies in flawed words and stubborn sounds.[81]

The poem that shatters the mirrors of appearance does so only by cooling into the shape of another mirror. There are no poems written wholly by necessity. To be drawn towards the ultimate union of being and meaning is not to arrive at a poem that cannot be deconstructed, but is to be inspired to produce works that, illusively, contingently, and always questionably, might *seem* to sail beyond the deferrals of language. This is the delight Stevens relates.

Do *all* poets begin romantically? Do all poets explicitly desire to write a wholly authentic poem? Such intense idealism cannot be assumed. What can be concluded, however, is that uncertainties are necessarily encountered in creativity, that these uncertainties cannot be entirely resolved, *and that attempts are nonetheless made to resolve them*. Redemption is not an experience of absolute completion – the closure is illusory, which is to say, fractional and circumstantial. Poems are written multiply, to use Hart's words, as "the necessarily accidental". Pure designs, tripped before they become such, emerge as contingent, partial reflections of what is unrepresentable. Uncertainty is not lessened, but moved into new and less exposed margins, later to be tapped as that threat to significance and signification that also offers scope for expressions not yet entertained. A poet does not choose uncertainty; he or she chooses, rather, to locate and respond to uncertainties that are always already available, becoming in the process (as-if-) responsible for what he or she can never master.

Interlude: Approaching Certainty

Imagine what it might mean to desire true love so strongly that the wish overtakes reality. The illusion cannot last. You are returned to the uncertainties amid which you will dream again.

Love on a Shoreline

She scatters sand from her palm, though
    the beach is miles away; she
doesn't notice. I let her speak into receding tides, and
    her words fall into oceans –
  it's one of those moments: her voice, as if
    robbed of its own source,
        dies
          and lives
            without distinction.

    I'd catch each grain, as it falls from her,
but nothing moves – time crumbles into
    shorelines,
  without land or sea.

        In another life,
      I alchemise each
       speck of sand
        into gold
         coins
       that I swap

for a serenading trumpet,
and we choose
between land
and water:
she leads me to where the trees
grow voices rich for troubadours:

we play... and we play...

But tides return: surf
tumbles into us, and
I haven't listened, and
she's never heard of any trumpet.
There's a pause, waves on
breaking rocks. We say we'll
meet again, it's been good, and she leaves
with
salt in ruffled hair.

Persuasion

"How is it possible," Blanchot asks, "to proceed with a firm step toward that which will not allow itself to be charted?"[82] The artist succeeds, Blanchot concludes, only by deceiving himself about what it is he does. Hence, in poetry, flawed words and stubborn sounds are offered as cogent expressions. Illusions are constructed over rumours of import, with the hope of effecting persuasion. The question addressed here is how such persuasion might be achieved. The task of writing is not one of surrender to unresolvable ambiguities, but one of speaking, arrogantly, if also tenuously, *as if* surrender were not necessary. "The work draws whoever devotes himself to it," Blanchot explains, "toward the point where it withstands its impossibility".[83] A work cannot dissolve its impossibility, but can be made to seem, in certain circumstances, to respond to uncertainty sufficiently. What counts as a sufficient response, and in which circumstances, are questions individual creators attempt to answer for each individual poem. The strategies that tend to be employed are equally multiple, but are not without pattern.

The technical and aesthetic contracts poets commit to in their efforts to produce persuasive poems, the forms they employ and the ideals they embrace, are discussed in detail in sections II and III. Themes and images, the concern of the current section, are also part of a poet's capacity for persuasion. Poets may draw, for example, on thematic sources of power perceived to be granted by cultural and disciplinary bias and by noteworthy events. There are no stated rules regarding the content of a poem, yet perceptions of relevance are inevitably contextual. War, to provide an obvious illustration, can command increased attention among poets and readers during times of conflict. Love and loss, more generally, tend to carry more poetic currency than, for example, scientific research or economic forecasts. Forbes' "Orange Sonnet" and Hejinian's *The Cell* (both quoted earlier) can also be seen to borrow force from (and give force to) the cultural interests that inform them. Both poems respond, in part, to the attention that has been given in the poststructural era to the notion that we are embedded in uncertainty. This can be said, too, for Kate Fagan's poem, "return to a new physics", which has us "pointing at nothing / as it empties". Fagan offers, in the same poem, "i write again, / signifying nothing sharp".[84] There is hypocrisy, surely, in seeking cogency from notions of uncertainty as if they were themselves certain. The contradiction is endured where the themes involved are perceived to be in other ways compelling, where their effects, in other words, can be seen to outweigh their internal entanglements. Fagan's poetry is far from dismissible. Its beauty surfaces in relation to its time; its internal entanglements contribute elegantly to an available argument.

Another way to effect persuasion in poetry is to openly lie. Donald Justice, in "The Artist Orpheus", writes:

> He might have sworn that he did not look back,
> That there was no one following on his track,
> Only the thing was that it made a better story
> To say that he had heard a sigh perhaps
> And once or twice the sound a twig makes when it snaps.[85]

On the back cover of the collection in which this poem appears, John Irving is quoted as saying:

39

The complexities of language have always been tempting to fakes; but while using fully the complexities of his language, Donald Justice has always demonstrated that the highest purpose of literature is to illuminate those things which are hard, disturbing, painful, moving, and repeat themselves – not to obscure them.

The comments complement each other well. Justice illuminates his concerns by telling good stories. That he manages to fabricate convincing relations in these stories (such as those between the artist Orpheus and his various loyalties) attests to his skill. It attests, also, to the licence given by the medium. It is not just that a poet may alter or invent materials to be used for a poem. The fabrication can be more overt, the metaphors can be ludicrous, the imagery exaggerated or impossible, and still, or *hence*, a poem may bear the potential to persuade. Gaston Bachelard, discussing his own view of the sources of power within poetry, suggests that "exaggeration is always at the summit of any living image".[86] It is incongruity, and not exaggeration alone, that can be enlivening. When Christopher Herold allows that, under a midnight moon, "a strip of eucalyptus bark / peels the silence",[87] incompatible terms construct a perceptual instability that is at once playful and earnest. The lie is presented as if it should bear meaning, and yet is literally senseless. The tension can be alluring. Raymond Roseliep's

> I tried to bring you
> that one cloud
> in this cup of water[88]

can effect comparable suspense, as can Forbes' "I am Cleopatra's dog / & my head is a balloon / of marsh gas rising from the Nile".[89] Countless illustrations are available. The suspense centres on the simultaneous presentation of purport and irrationality, of sincerity and absurdity – the poems flaunt deviance amid their claims of cogency. How is the combination persuasive?

Incongruity in poetry, the trace of a poet's exposure to a Derridean threshold (where things can be infinitely other), is pursued for the intensity it can deliver. Incongruities stand out both by seeming unusual and by needing to be resolved: each conspicuous slide towards unreadability requests its own rescue. The risk is that the request will pass unanswered. Where rescue is deemed possible, however, the poem concerned can be seen to achieve apparently *im*possible signification. Relevance can be established *as if in spite of* the work itself. Recklessness can seem to visibly transmute into understanding, and the poet and the poem are shown to have the strength to entertain both. The arrival of meaning can yield, here, feelings of surprise and relief, not necessarily because the meaning is itself surprising or reassuring, but because its availability was in question. This involvement can be increased by the sense that the meaning drawn from incongruity can seem to have a source other than the words through which it is formed. To deliver import through nonsensicality, to effect representation through overt *mis*-representation, is to emphasise that it is not words themselves that achieve understanding. Words, we are reminded, are in service to something other than language, something, says the romantic, more profound, more pure, and something, says the poet, that cannot be translated into prose. Immediacy and experientiality in poetic expression can be induced via what is effectively a request for imaginative participation. The risks, to repeat, are significant. Herold's and Roseliep's haiku (both quoted above) are unsuccessful unless their readers feel able to complete for themselves each abbreviated scene. Incongruity, then, increases the possibility that a poem will seem inaccessible. The risk is taken for the chance that where meaning is gleaned, the intensity and allure given to it by the means of delivery will render it all the more compelling.

Is it fair to refer to the incongruities poets employ as lies? They are not generally called such: "rhetorical device" and "figure of speech" are more common terms. Their appeal resides, potentially, in their violation and renewal of accepted associations. It resides, too, in the entry they can seem to grant into a more immediate, less textual experience of a (nonetheless textual) poem. Such invigoration is called for in Victor Shklovsky's notion of defamiliarisation. Here, a "roughened language" is ideally to break our attention from what we believe we know and to induce participation in an intense "noticing" of as-if-newly-encountered subjects.[90] Art exists, Shklovsky writes,

> that one may recover the sensation of life; it exists to make one feel things, to make the stone *stony*. The purpose of art is to impart the sensation of things as they are perceived and not as they are known. The technique of art is to make objects 'unfamiliar', to make forms difficult, to increase the difficulty and length of perception because the process of perception is an aesthetic end in itself and must be prolonged.[91]

Incongruity is a player, a tool, in the project of defamiliarisation. It is indeed a means of teasing perception towards renewed awareness. Yet the term "lie" remains appropriate. To the quotation given above, Shklovsky adds, in italics, that *"Art is a way of experiencing the artfulness of an object; the object is not important"*.[92] Poetic contracts, to return to an earlier argument, may be given priority over the personal experiences that inform them. The statements are the same. The objects, feelings, and events that become the subjects of a poem are unquestionably important, for the poem is nothing without them, yet the poem is also nothing if it does not aspire to become something else, a persuasive experience in its own right. It cannot be the objects, feelings, and events themselves. At best, it can induce an effect whereby the gap between itself and its (variously transformed) subjects appears to close, or diminish. The effect is necessarily an illusion. To experience the artfulness of an object is to embrace this illusion. This is where the lie resides.

A redeeming poem lifts us from our entrapment in textuality, from our entrapment, that is, in the conditions and absences that allow signs to be signs, by speaking energetically and persuasively (a consoling celebration) *within* that textuality.[93] Words are distrusted in literature, Blanchot tells us, yet this distrust takes the form not of wordlessness, but of heightened word play and increased ambiguity.[94] Redemption can arise, indeed, from contrivance and textual play. In literature, Blanchot explains, "deceit and mystification not only are inevitable but constitute the writer's honesty, whatever hope and truth are in him".[95] Incongruity, we might say, is the exploitation of an absence (of strict signifiers) performed to create a presence. As a poetic lie, it is a trick sincerely forged and is aptly named.

Interlude: Provocative Lies

Poetic lies are not the simple products of creativity. They are part of the creative process. The initial comparison may begin a more elaborate exploration. The fit of the subject may become a source of excitement, an inducement, also a commitment. Discipline and care guard against over-excitement and misplaced commitment. From the licence of the lie, a whole, living creature is ideally born.

Caving: a translation

Attempting throughways
from distant ends, tunnels
in the sprawl of air, loud
with our own noise, our eyes,
blind in the dark curve,
lending fingers, feet, elbows,
to stony folds, while the black
strokes beyond the skin, we're
listening for more than echoes.

Caves come out, you're a
matchstick flare, and I'm
fumbling for navigation.

Conclusion

A poet experiences creative redemption by transforming subjective impressions into what he or she perceives to be persuasive, poetic expression. His or her personal influence can seem to become part of a community of ideas and artefacts (the poems themselves). The process involves recognition of and a response to multiple uncertainties, uncertainties that are never permanently settled. A redeeming work is achieved both because of and in spite of these uncertainties. They are the challenge and scope by which conventions can be revised and augmented, and they are the threat of insignificance that is to be (re-)negotiated via methods of persuasion. The perceived appeal of a created work can affirm, for a poet, what the invitation to uncertainty effectively threatens, namely his or her and the medium's capacity for new and significant poetry. Opportunities for such redemption require specific poetic, personal, and social contexts. It is in these contexts, and, more specifically, through the contracts poets establish within them, that uncertainties become perceivable and that concerted efforts towards persuasiveness can be made. In poetry, technical and aesthetic contracts allow uncertainty to be accessed and responded to through a process that is at once constraining *and* liberating. This is the argument attended to in sections II (technical constraints) and III (aesthetic constraints).

Intermission: Translation

Uncertainty occupies the distance between words and subjects. A poem can reflect but cannot be what it depicts. Redemption lies in the sense that this distance has been disguised. The poem becomes elegiac, celebrating a capacity for expression even as it declares itself to be a substitute for what it cannot hold.

Night Swim

moon

                trunks

       ripple

                   into hearing –

blackwoods,   gums…

              my own

      limbs

           cobweb

        in tissues

                 of the

      water's cold,

       and flowers

          in the blackwood's

     arms

  float

        scent

        filled

            with darkness

   into   pores

of the night's

     hollow skin.

Aurora

> space dust melts into psychedelic juice,
>   the south sky wobbles off its dome,
> bruising into flames,
>   as if its ribs
> peel and the heart
>   bleeds into patchwork:
> red green red green –
>   a shadowed cloth
>   we roll under pillows
>   to dream in the night's skull.

cello concerto
          (Schumann, cello concerto in A minor)

like voltage, promising escape:
dendrites tensed by the cello's bow
pulse in the heart's thermals;
there are burn marks
inside the cheekbones;

and nothing resolves: recall
plunders the melody –
a hummingbird momentum
holding the lungs.

Painting, 1810
The promise of more than passing

Gum-tips scribble long librettos
on a glassed-in page

and the wind's wild tongue,
slowed by the painter's brush,

is almost audible,
caught on a moon's edge

where it holds its fleeting strength
against irrelevance. All hope

strains to feel the swell
spill beyond its frame: you touch

the long vowels, and seeing,
too, is hearing:

from the gums,
an aria of endurance.

intimacy

yielding one where
two might have walked away.

Beside me

facing his back, his sleep leaning between us, I'm in the fields of his
mottled skin, and I can see but can't touch, dissolving
from his front-of-body, the silk light of his being;

his heat settles in my fingers, and through the rise and fall
of his chest's circling winds, I hold
what I cannot hold – his mute warmth spreads

through the gridlock of his spine, and I press
with fluid hands, nearing
what the day cannot deliver.

Threading the Moon

just a baby: the shadowed skin
of its fontanelle.

```
                    t
                  he
              slo
          w ic
        e of
        its s
          ton
            y e
              dg
                  e
```

                    b
                  re
                    ath
                        mar
                        k o
                        f t
                    he
                  su
            n

no vapour
from its white dissolve: lost
in its china poise:

   an immaculate blue.

Ligeti, smiling
                    (String Quartet No.2)

between his notes, a stretching of ligatures,
such that she's startled by

influx round a fracture
in the solid workings of common sense.

She wraps resistance
across the wound, remembering

rest and compression make
for a speedier recovery, but she

wonders if it's safe
enough to be

unsafe… peels back an edge
to see the extent of the injury:

sky shifts from its easy blue
and she looks from where he looks, right

through her.

Section II: Constraints

The Form of Freedom

Poets gain licence for taking risks in their creative endeavours by agreeing to produce works that, to a sufficient extent, resemble poems. In this section, focus is given to the effect on creativity of a poet's commitment to poetic forms and techniques. The suggestion is that opportunities for creativity, and the uncertainties that fuel these opportunities, can be accessed and intensified via constraints relating to technical conventions in poetry. Importantly, while technical contracts are to reflect, in part, a commitment to existing networks of meaning, there is no ultimate authority regarding what a poet's technical contracts should look like or how they might be satisfied. A poet responds to uncertainty using technical contracts as a frame and a location, but must also respond to uncertainty *within* these same agreements; there are no transcendental guidelines on how to write poetry. Through their malleability, technical contracts can themselves become the objects of a poet's creativity. New forms and techniques can be invented and old ones modified. Technical contracts, then, can both focus and become the focus of a poet's creative intentions. The second chapter of this section examines how technical contracts function in the creation of individual poems. The third chapter considers the effect of importing contractual constraints from other creative fields. Cross-discipline exchange, it is argued, can licence expression in poetry that poetic contracts alone cannot support. The fourth chapter summarises the part technical contracts play in creative redemption, attending particularly to the relations between constraint and uncertainty in poetic creativity. More immediately, in this opening chapter, the concern is to outline the broad, characterising features of the technical contracts poets employ.

Creativity becomes possible and meaningful relative to specific frames of reference. "Regardless of the period at which we look," Arthur Koestler writes, "every work of art betrays the prejudiced eye, governed by selective codes which lend coherence to the artist's vision, and at the same time restrict his freedom".[96] By adopting selective codes, individuals become able to organise and communicate their thoughts. Codes that describe the prejudices of poetic conventions favour those organisations of thought known as poetry. The need to learn and to apply these codes has been heavily emphasised by a number of poets. "The spirit of poetry," writes Samuel Taylor Coleridge, "like all other living powers, must of necessity circumscribe itself by rules".[97] Frank Kermode is more brutal: "Theoretical contempt for form in the arts," he exclaims, "is a fraud".[98] David Lehman states that, "Without the resistance of a chosen medium, there can be no art, for art abhors anarchy".[99] Art does not *wholly* abhor anarchy. The uncertainties encountered in creativity can effectively invite its arrival, and the taste or hint of chaos can become alluring both as an escape from established forms and as the chance to construct other kinds of order. There is no allure, however, in chaos alone: pure anarchy would leave no means by which alluring hints might be detected and responded to. It is as Wallace Stevens concludes: "To be at the end of fact is not to be at the beginning of the imagination but it is to be at the end of both".[100] One needs clarities, A.R. Ammons suggests, "to know what one is baffled by".[101] Rules, facts, clarities, and resistances are all a form of bias. They ensure that a range of possibilities pass unnoticed. Yet the alternative is to arrive at a point of what Blanchot calls "extreme poverty" and "infinite idleness", where

> inspiration, this movement outside of tasks, of acquired forms and proven expressions, takes the name aridity and becomes the absence of power, the impossibility which the artist questions in vain...[102]

A technical contract is the discipline a poet accepts as a way of directing and supporting his or her will to create.

But how do forms and resistances contain the threat of anarchy and aridity without inhibiting creativity? Again, it is the comments of creators themselves that offer insight. Igor Stravinsky, referring to creativity in music, is exuberant in his insistence that,

> My freedom will be so much the greater and more meaningful, the more narrowly I limit my field of action and the more I surround myself with obstacles. Whatever diminishes constraints, diminishes strength. The more constraints one imposes, the more one frees one's self of the chains that shackle the spirit.[103]

John Ashbery, equivalently, explains that his interest in the pantoum rose from "its stricture, even greater than in other hobbling forms such as the sestina or canzone. These restraints seem to have a paradoxically liberating effect, for me at least".[104] Richard Kenney, too, refers to "the liberating manacles of formal poetry".[105] It is not the pantoum, the sestina, or the canzone that can liberate a poet, but the act of tackling and overcoming a particular challenge. Any technical contract to which a poet is committed, including the apparently loose form of (so-called) free verse, will offer constraints of some kind. Different constraints will be found more or less appealing depending on the poet and the poem. They are appealing, primarily, for what it is they expose. By narrowing the context in which creativity happens, the "manacles of poetry" facilitate greater heed. Specific problems in need of specific responses become available, and intense concentration can be achieved, which may itself be invigorating. Constraints in creativity, importantly, are to limit a creator's *field* of action, but not action itself. A contract does not remove the need for choice, but rather amplifies that need, rendering it urgent, even, as a response to identified difficulties. Obstacles liberate by giving poets the opportunity to direct their powers to tangible sites of potential influence. This direction may threaten even as it lends possibility to the expression of specific impressions, yet this conflict is itself part of the challenge that is sought.

The particular nature of the technical contract employed in the creation of a poem will reflect the interests and skills of the poet concerned and the culture of the time and place of writing. The appeal of certain forms and methods, and of the possibility of revising those forms and methods, is partly a function of circumstance. Several relatively stable elements of the technical contracts poets tend to embrace can nonetheless be identified. The logic of poetry, or logics, for there are many kinds of poetry, change as new works and styles are developed, but do so relative to a number of fundamental concerns. Perhaps the most basic concern sustained by poets is that for sound. Koestler observes that, "the poet creates by bisociating sound and sense, metre and meaning".[106] The description is a summary of Paul Valéry's comment (quoted by Koestler, from Valéry's "The Course in Poetics") that poets

> must simultaneously obey perfectly incongruous conditions: musical, rational, significant, and suggestive; conditions which require a continuous and repeated connection between

rhythm and syntax, between *sound* and *sense*... the coupling of the *phonetic variable* with the *semantic variable* creates problems of extension and convergence which poets solve blindfold – but they solve them (and this is the essential thing), from time to time.[107]

Sound is written into poetic contracts as a necessary contributor to the conceptual and emotional meaning a poem delivers. The poet, says Louis Zukofsky, "looks, so to speak, into his ear as he does at the same time into his heart and intellect".[108] The concern for sound provides a source of problems that are, in turn, opportunities for creative solutions. They are *additional* problems, what *The New Princeton Encyclopedia of Poetry and Poetics* terms "excess pattern".[109] The call for rhythm, for example, inserts a contrived complexity that requires numerous potentially creative decisions to be made, decisions regarding line lengths, pace and metre, stanzaic form, and so on. Even in prose poetry, these concerns remain significant: a pseudo or teased lineation effects hesitations and repetitions within sentences that consequently still need to be quoted as they appear in print, with line endings unchanged. Whether a poet commits to iambic pentameter or to free verse, to a syllabic count or to the "breath" in a poem's lines (where, according to Charles Olson, the energy of one's breath is to be transformed into language and recorded typographically[110]), apparently unnecessary constraints are introduced. The poem being written is given direction, but it is a direction that adds to, even as it begins to answer, the problem of translating an impression into poetry.

Beside rhythm, there is an expectation, equally fundamental, for rhyme, and if not direct rhyme, then near rhyme, assonance, alliteration, and other aural repetitions. The patterning here can also be kinaesthetic and visual: what the ear detects may be sensed, as well, and amplified, by the mouth, through actual or imagined utterances, and by the eye, through visual resemblances. Such echoes are evident in comparisons between "needle" and "neglect", "tongue" and "longer", "sky" and "rhythm", "crude roar" and "rupture", and between "chilled", "stanched", and "mends". Contracts in rhyme allow otherwise innocent elements of everyday speech to become sources of friction and possibility. Consonants and vowels are embraced, in poetry, as degrees of freedom that allow additional forms of expression, and as constraints that, since the influence given to their sound cannot consequently be ignored, refuse the option of a "soundless" poem. Form, to repeat, liberates even as it binds. Punctuation, too, can be given heightened and contractual significance, as exemplified in the work of Dickinson and cummings. The use of white space and silence in a poem, via, for example, staggered and broken lines, can also become relevant. None of these variables are given attention in isolation, and the problem of how to meaningfully integrate a poem's multiple components offers further opportunities for creativity.

Technical contracts draw poets into a discipline through which works that look and sound like poems can be created. Each contract will reflect a poet's commitment to a range of poetic conventions, through which particular rhythms and rhymes are able to be meaningfully negotiated. What follows from this, and what is pursued in the next chapter, is the question of how such contracts operate in the production of specific poems.

Interlude: Taking Shape

The willingness to allow material to be worked on as an element of a poetic rather than, or as well as, a personal reality, can be aided by the emergence of and a commitment to a particular shape and sound. Rhythms and sound patterns can establish a poem as a distinct entity and remove it from the sense that it is simply a record of an impression. A recollection of one moment thus becomes an artwork with an independent "life", one that must arrive at many moments if its readers are to each gain access to its moods and meanings. A poem's emerging shape contributes, in other words, to a process of objectification whereby concern can be given not only for the material employed, but for the impact and the completeness of the poem itself. "Faith" offers a story that can no longer be told (without significant alteration) within the context of casual conversation. The anecdote with which it began is no longer owned by a personal voice; it has been openly translated. If anything, it is owned, now, by the poetic sounds and forms that hold it together.

Faith

Seeds erupt from the air's pores,
caught in teasing winds, like hooped skirts

twirling over open fields.
I climb, touching nothing,

floating over charged ground, a small figure
lost in the wind's arms. The sky

finds its way
through the limits of my fingers.

The Act of Writing

A technical contract is not a settled document but, rather, part of an ongoing response by a poet to a selected subject, to the emerging poem, and to the wider poetic community. The effect of a technical contract, even if it alters during the writing process, is to both support and provoke creative decision-making. The question is how. Molly Peacock illustrates how contracts can *support* poetic creativity by describing the writing process behind her poem, "She Lays", a sonnet on masturbation. "Facing a blank page," Peacock explains,

> I felt it would be impossible to make up the shape of self-love as I went along. How could this frail subject make its own clumsy masonry? So I chose a 'form' as a vehicle to take me to this intimate place. Instead of bewilderment, I chose limitation. The limitations of the lines then became long corridors to freedom... Having everywhere at my disposal, I would not have known where to go.[111]

For Peacock, the sonnet lent specificity to an amorphous problem. Containment offered by a specific form may also have licensed daring for John Tranter in his writing of *Crying in Early Infancy: 100 Sonnets*, though here the daring extends to a teasing of the form itself. The work's poems move backwards and forwards across a boundary of rational sense, approaching, in places (as sonnet 20 explains), "a catalogue of dreams / just like my life".[112] Limits of meaning are finely explored, and the familiar poetic structure Tranter employs (and mildly renegotiates) becomes the ground against which this exploration gains coherency. Smaller elements of poetic form can offer equivalent support. For Alan Williamson, secure metre in a poem grants permission: "It draws a kind of magic circle", Williamson writes, "within which, as in primitive cultures, it is safe to dance out one's possession by the demon".[113] Williamson and Tranter can be compared here not for the kinds of poems they produce or for the reasons they write them, but for the freedom each finds in particular technical contracts. Robert Creeley, too, recalling Pound's claim that "Verse consists of a constant and a variant",[114] describes how the quatrain provided, for a time, the stability he felt he needed; the variant, he explains, could then occur in the line. Poetic forms can render a poet safe enough to be unsafe. The direction gained can allow risks to be taken regarding other aspects of the poem being written. Pinned from the slide into aridity (to use Blanchot's term), a poet may become able to entertain otherwise unapproachable uncertainties.

Creativity can also be directly provoked by a poet's technical contracts. Ammons suggests we need "precipitations of forms / to use like tongs against the formless".[115] Robert Brown, in *The Handbook of Creativity*, argues that "one needs an observable guide to the unobservable".[116] Technical contracts can be observable guides, goads, even, to what has not yet been conceived of or fully realised; they can incite effort in ways that expose new and unexpected opportunities for expression. A poet's technique, writes Seamus Heaney "involves the discovery of ways to go out of his normal cognitive bounds and raid the inarticulate".[117] There are no ultimate answers as to how such "raids" are to be achieved – chance encounters, non-poetic interests, and sustained reflection may all be influential, in conjunction with *or despite* a poet's technical engagements. Technical contracts, however, do bear the potential to provide a means of approaching and of coaxing into existence things un- and half-imagined. It is a claim many poets reiterate. Anthony Hecht argues that through formal considerations a poet "will be invited to discover meanings or implications he had never considered before. In this way the 'unforeseen' emerges from the small germ of the beginning".[118] Richard Kenney, too, referring to the pleasures of rhyme, writes:

> One, in the hearing, is obvious; the other, in the making, has to do with a kind of random or irrational search, a momentary crippling of the intellect, looking for words according to sound rather than sense. It's a practical tool for finding what you don't know you're looking for, as the expression goes – what sometimes comes to perfect sense".[119]

A technical contract raises difficulties that need not be associated with a poem's subjects. They are difficulties responded to, however, with these subjects in mind, and it is this crossing of influences that can release unexpected possibilities. It can be surprisingly beneficial, as Richard Wilbur explains, to "put yourself in a position where you have to pay attention to all sorts of wild suggestions which come to you through the sound contract you have made".[120]

A poet's sources of stability and provocation will change from one poem to another. Different kinds of contracts will, further, suit different kinds of poets. David Lehman, referring to poets as problem solvers, writes that, "By this logic, the tougher the formal problem, the better – the more likely it is to act as a sort of broker between language, chance, and the poet's instincts".[121] Toughness, though, is an inadequate measure of a contract's conduciveness to creativity. A constraint one poet finds invigorating may seem too awkward or forced to another. A contract that is sufficiently challenging in one context may appear uninteresting in other situations. Peacock contrasts formal poetic structures, which she describes as "a way of braving an emotion's universe", with free verse. The latter, she writes, does not provide the same facilitation, appearing instead as "millions of small decisions in chaos" which "have about them a sense of overwhelming struggle".[122] The comment reflects Peacock's particular bias rather than the form itself, as is evidenced by the large number of poets for whom the "overwhelming struggle" is both engaging and generative. Free verse, despite its name, offers potentially supportive and provocative constraints. Sound and sense must still convincingly intersect, and the absence of a strict framing pattern (as provided by sonnets, pantoums, and the like) can expose smaller *emerging* patterns (in sound, syntax, appearance, and so on). Commitment is given in part to relations that become apparent *during* the act of writing. William Stafford records his preference for forms that surface as he works: "There is no name for them," he comments, "but as the poem develops it becomes full of incipient patterns, little places you can pet and bring along".[123] The patterns a writer of free verse develops will still reflect perceived notions of what constitutes a poem and of what constitutes free verse. As for more formal poetry, these selected codes can seem severe enough to liberate departures from conventional thinking. Stafford writes that,

> The areas of experiment, of exploration, of discovery, are those areas that have to do with the language experience that forces you to make leaps that you ordinarily wouldn't make. All sorts of little enticements show up in the syllables and in the pace of the phrasing, with the way the sequences go in the sentence and the alternatives that begin to occur to you.[124]

Direction and unexpected stimulation can both arise, in free verse, from a commitment to informal rhythms and rhymes.

Technical contracts are only useful by virtue of a poet's capacity to perceive and respond to the problems and freedoms they offer. At certain times, and for certain poets, the direct use of an existing model of poetry, formal *or* "free", may seem more onerous or mundane than liberating. Stimulation can require a radical choice of constraints, a break, that is, from the norm and an insertion of a contract that seems both more modern and challenging. Technical contracts are always in some way specific to individual poems. The point here is that the act of tailoring a contract to one's own needs can at times escalate into major innovation. e.e. cummings, once again, provides a clear example. cummings adapted poetic and grammatical norms to produce a self-styled contract to which he remained committed through much of his work. That it was a contract and not anarchic subversion is reflected in the consistency of his distinctive style and in the general acceptance of that style as something poetic. Excess pattern, added to by the importance given by cummings to individual letters, to "misplaced" capitalisation, and to "erroneous" punctuation, allows, in the poems, new ways of drawing attention to and of recasting otherwise ordinary words and meanings. cummings writes, for example,

D-re-A-mi-N-gl-Y

leaves
(sEe)
locked

in

gOLd
after-
gLOw

are

t
ReMbLiN
g

,;:..:;, [125]

The act of negotiating a technical contract can, then, involve as well as induce intense creativity. cummings, importantly, at no stage rejects poetry itself. His poems play earnestly with traditional meaning structures, *almost* sacrificing coherency, and celebrating, implicitly, the medium that permits them to do so. The works reflect a general property of technical innovation in the field. Dislocation of a poetic norm will have, unless the poet concerned is to cease writing poetry, a subplot of poetic perpetuation. The subplot is that which licenses and locates a poet's creative effort.

A further example of marked technical innovation is provided by the (loosely grouped) Beat poets of the 1950s and 60s. The Beat poets expressed a desire for liberation from what were perceived to be irrelevant and excessive restrictions, in politics as well as poetry. "Spontaneity" was favoured over tradition. Yet the shared urge for greater freedom and individuality was identifiable only through significant agreement regarding what that freedom and individuality might look like. Preferences emerged for a certain kind of pitch, inflection, gesture, and pace, and for "unfinished" or open forms, including improvised performances. Allen Ginsberg's "Howl" provides an example. In effect, the new contracts were no less severe than the traditions that were rejected. Amiri Baraka, a poet associated with the movement, exclaims,

> I *must* be completely free to do just what I want, in the poem. "All is permitted": Ivan's crucial concept. There cannot be anything I must *fit* the poem into. Everything must be made to fit into the poem. There must not be any preconceived notion or *design* for what the poem ought to be.[126]

Baraka's efforts, of course, were *designed* to satisfy his particular poetic bias and were not "completely free" at all – "must", "crucial", "cannot", and "ought" are not the words of a liberated poet. I must be completely free, Baraka writes, *"in the poem"* – I want to diverge from the dominant conventions, Baraka means, without ceasing to be a poet. The freedom experienced by the Beat poets did not lie in the forms and ideals they espoused, but in the extent to which they were able to renegotiate existing poetic (and political) conditions *without losing the capacity to write poetry*. Such freedom can be gained, theoretically, in response to any existing convention. It is unavailable, ironically, to a poet (poetically suicidal) who avoids convention altogether. In any field, revolution requires a platform from which revision can be attempted.

Technical contracts can support and provoke poetic creativity, and can themselves become a site of innovation. They cannot guarantee the creation of a rewarding poem, nor will any particular contract seem appealing to all poets. Language Poets, like other innovators, have sought new problems and obstacles through which to diverge from existing styles of writing. Assumptions that have shaped poetry in the past have been questioned, and distinctive and novel responses have been developed for the uncertainties accordingly unleashed. The legitimacy and appeal both of the techniques and of the poems that follow from them have been variously perceived. Eliot Weinberger is not alone when he rejects what he describes as "an endless succession of depthless images and empty sounds, each cancelling the previous one".[127] Poetries based on chance procedures and on systematic text-generating methods, where constraint construction can become the main concern (if not the sole creative act), also illustrate the potential for disagreement. Enthusiasm from some (writers of Oulipian poetry and Computer poetry, for example) contrasts with rejection (or indifference) from others. What is liberating for one poet, what stretches expression and breaks habitual thinking, can seem, to another, distasteful, limiting, or irrelevant. New possibilities for meaning can seem to be tapped or, by the same technique, blocked, depending on the individuals and the circumstances involved.

Interlude: Emerging Patterns, I

A single line can begin a sound pattern, a pace, and a tone that is at once a frame for writing and a problem in need of a solution. The support and provocation inherent in even this apparently simple initial contract is sufficient to drive the creative act forward. As further lines are written, and as all lines and stanzas are edited, the contract may be extensively revised, each alteration becoming an equal part in the response to the challenge of writing. Guided by *emerging* contracts in sound and shape, a poet may not arrive at what appear to be the fundamental structures of the final poem (such as whether it is written in quatrains or couplets) until quite late in the writing process. "flow" began with short lines and no stanza breaks, its mood being established by the lines, "Arriving home / While she slept" and, later in the poem, "I peeled daylight / From where it lingered / Against my skin".

flow

I arrive home while she sleeps; the day
peels from where it lingers on my skin

and in the half-warmth of our bed,
I feel her heat steal over me:

like sliding through the outline of my own name,
lifting to where she slumbers.

I let her go, "wife", "lover", "woman",
and we are cheekbones and quiet breath,

a melt of ribs, ever rising. In the morning,
we rescue words

from the shores
of night-time's flow.

Emerging Patterns, II

A poem can be strongly shaped by a commitment to a specific tempo. Three words (such as "in no mood") may be sufficient to establish an apparently urgent and insistent technical contract. To satisfy the design that emerges to meet this contract, words may need to be sought that would otherwise not have been considered. The sound of three words, then, can be enough to draw the support and provocation required to begin a poem.

in no mood

I'm in no mood to cut (she says to – why?); she says to
cut things up – what does she mean, *she*,
the gut reply, the foot's arch: because she's tied?
Cut? At the risk of losing … what? A hand? A
heart? Cut loose? No mood for loose. Or perhaps
a rearrangement. Cut, as if to
make, or to re-make, to redeem. So what
she *doesn't* say – cut things up, a kind of (does she
mean) chance for (in a yes mood) putting things together.
Is that what it takes? Can't make first? cut later?
    The cut's made. And the edges, like when
hair, pulled to snapping, snaps, jerk back. There's

space. And a struggle: someone's hand
out of reach, unattached. Track marks in a desert
start and end where I stand. I'm in
no (I'd say mood, but it's gone beyond that) no
state of (cut up, bleeding) mind. But there's

    still life, a sinkhole, thumb-sized, something
burrowing under sand. Do I (one-handed) dig?
I wait. Night falls. She says to cut, and I'm in no

mood, so I (what can I say) make room, and the gap
means (doesn't it?) something builds, like

  morning, only slower. Cut? To cut things.
To make whole, one way or another. There are
mouse bones, come sunrise, in the hollow.
She says to pull (to pull *apart*) each bone, but I
tell her I can't: they've scurried off, they're
in the sand dunes, fossicking with a
force of their own, not quite expected. She says...
but I tell her I'm leaving. She's

  kicked back onto the left heel as I
stumble. I tell her I'm
                cured.

Cross-discipline Constraints

Poetic contracts can be influenced by materials that are distinctly non-poetic. The hybridity already present in poetry, that between sense and sound, can in this way be extended. Forms and techniques may be imported from any number of fields and cultures, and while there is no promise that the crossover will be invigorating, the possibility exists. Modern dithyrambs, pantoums, haiku, tanka, and the like, each the result of a fusion between poetries of different times and places, have proven stimulating for a number of poets. In the crossbred genre of prose poetry, the intersection is of a different kind, offering, rather than fusion, ongoing opposition. The competing forms co-exist, licensing contracts for a peculiar kind of creativity that settles neither into prose nor into poetry. Lineation, rhythm, and rhyme are as-if-but-not-quite thwarted, as-if-but-not-quite usurpative. To accept the challenge to write neither poetry nor prose, while writing both, is to accept permission to write something "other". The contract(s) will still need to be in some way satisfied – the liberation the crossover effects is conditional – yet possibilities unique to the form can also be uncovered. Fictocriticism, in which multiple generic threads may merge (poetry among them), facilitates and exploits comparable cross-fertilisation. A creator's notions of what can be said, and how, are potentially augmented.

Intense exchanges can also take place between poetry and literary theory. Since in one, words are carefully put together to achieve particular effects, while in the other, careful attention is given to *how* words might achieve particular effects, the intersection is to be expected. Poets who take no direct interest in literary theory's accounts of the mechanisms of writing are still likely to be influenced by developments in the field. Cultural prevalence can make certain perspectives and approaches difficult to avoid. Coleridge, Eliot, and Hejinian are poets whose interests in how words mean can be clearly related to the times in which each was and is writing. Coleridge's "organic unity", Eliot's concern for cultural memory and embedded symbolism, and Hejinian's associative play are romantic, modern, and post-modern respectively. Exchanges between poetry and literary theory reflect, then, the closeness of these fields within the society generally, though intersections may also be actively sought by particular poets. Poetry and philosophy are similarly intertwined. Less dense cross-discipline exchanges are also noteworthy. Fred D'Aguiar describes a dialogue between the fields of poetry and history as being, for him, particularly important. He records finding provocation in historical constraints: "I functioned best," D'Aguiar explains,

> when locked into a particular historical dilemma. My imagination plunged into the history of its environment even as it sought to surface from it and leave it behind for a space not governed by any social or historical predicament. ... It is as if history were the parent that the imagination had to acknowledge every time as it fled to a place of its own making.[128]

Music has also been recognised by many poets as a potent hybridising force. Parallel concerns (for tone and rhythm) intensify the exchange. "Music has given me a much greater sense of the possibilities of quantity in poetry", James Wright notes.[129] For Laurie Duggan, the merge is almost subliminal: "I'm not technically up there," Duggan states, "but I would be surprised if certain elements of music which I like, such as the drone or kinds of modality, didn't infuse the work".[130] Musical forms and techniques, Duggan implies, can contribute to a poet's technical contract.

Why are such exchanges attractive? The challenge of solving a new set of problems and the opportunity to create using new materials without leaving one's chosen field, are reasons enough. Borrowed methods and meanings may at times also bring with them allusions to an established authority or appeal. An extreme example is given by the partnership between poetry and psychoanalysis. Surrealistic and other avant-garde poetries of the 1920s gained many of their characteristics from methods and principles that psychoanalysis was bringing to public attention. New procedures (automatic writing, for instance) were cultivated from notions made not merely available but also pressing by Freud's hugely influential work. Psychoanalysis provided the Surrealist poets with an unexplored, apparently defensible, and contemporary reference through which to develop fresh approaches to writing. Kevin Brophy, discussing the exchange between creative writing and psychoanalysis, and referring specifically to the poet André Breton, writes that, "the discovery of the unconscious was the discovery of a technique".[131] It was a technique both sufficiently supported and sufficiently daring to attract (and to still attract) the attention of creators across many fields.

The potential benefits to creativity arising from cross-discipline exchange prompt the behavioural theorist, Robert Epstein to exclaim: "Learn something entirely different! ... The new will interconnect with the old in novel and potentially fascinating ways".[132] John Hayes, in *The Handbook of Creativity*, is more explicit:

> A unique pattern of knowledge outside of a field, which is acquired perhaps through hobbies or through switching professions, could provide a person with analogies that are not generally available to others in the field. Such analogies could suggest unexpected possibilities or problems in the field.[133]

Through exchanges between disciplines, cognitive norms can be unsettled and new means of expression can emerge. A creator's awareness of his or her chosen field may be simultaneously heightened through an exposure of those qualities that distinguish it from each intersecting domain. There is no rule to say which materials might most usefully be imported, for even apparently obscure connections can add dimensions to a creator's resources. The composer Morton Feldman illustrates the point by describing the influence of his interest in Near and Middle Eastern rugs: "Rugs have prompted me in my recent music to think of a disproportionate symmetry," Feldman writes, "in which a symmetrically staggered rhythmic series is used: 4:3, 6:5, 8:7, etc., as the point of departure".[134]

Is it to be concluded, here, that broad and contrasting interests should be consciously developed by creators? Might the pursuit of multiple projects enhance an individual's creativity? Colin Martindale, in a study of personality and circumstance in creativity, asserts that "the more diverse and general a person's store of ideas, the greater is the chance that a creative idea will emerge".[135] The comment requires the strict proviso that access to specific tools, through which the general store of ideas might be usefully sifted and reassembled, *also* exists. General information on its own is insufficient for creativity, and if acquiring diverse general knowledge means sacrificing the development of specialist skills, the benefits become questionable. To be in a position to be challenged by alternatives and to encounter provocative crossovers is to have established a commitment to a discipline within which these alternatives and provocations might seem significant. "Clearly," writes Epstein, "different experiences make a big difference in creative performances, but there's more to creativity than experience". Epstein emphasises that what is essential in creativity is the will and the means to unravel, manipulate, and re-amalgamate the knowledge that is available.[136] Non-poetic influences in poetry achieve little without the sense of relevance and direction that is conferred by the will and means to write poems.

Interlude: Jazz

A desire to respond in poetry to the work of other artists can effect a license for a new kind of writing. Mimicry and open influence can allow new rhythms and word choices to displace other personal and poetic tendencies. The cross-over can be invigorating. (Wynton Marsalis is a US jazz trumpeter, born in 1962.)

The Line   (after Wynton Marsalis)

A player drops notes in a broken field, and I knock them into furrows,
to let them sit, but they won't stop still. He's got a line going, and it
bends a little, easing friction from its silky sway, hustling for its quiet ride.
Notes sink rifts into dogged time, and years slip from the player's line:
dee-li-dee, dee-ahh, a line that binds: dee-li-dee
    And he has me, gives a little, takes a little, ploughs a little deeper,
and the shake is at the heart's core – I'm quivering. Notes hurl into
hollow limbs: doo-la-doo, la-dee, and he's cruising: doo-ba-doo di, di, di...
gives it to me, pinning me, holding me, inside, and he leans, embracing me,
gaoling me: doo-ba doo-ba di-loo
                      ba-di-da, ba-di-doo, ba-di-day... and all
the while playing, him and me, one field, the same, thinking: dee-li-dee,
and working, dee-ahh... ba-di-ahh; *gives* it to me, one more time, and we're
swinging, sliding into midnight, each note, breaking into smooth, and its
smoky rise
                dealing the addiction.
                                      ... Dawn
                                    rolls over us.

Constraints and Redemption

Creativity in poetry requires some use of existing conventions. What has been argued is that this use can facilitate and goad the act of writing. Established forms and techniques, those of poetry, unavoidably, and those imported from other fields, if such exchanges take place, provide a location and direction for creative endeavour, even when the forms themselves are heavily revised. What they do not and cannot provide is a complete escape from convention. The idea of a *necessary* deference to existing means and methods causes the composer Morton Feldman to insist that "everything we use to make art is precisely what kills it".[137] Referring to his development of a distinct musical notation, one that introduces alternative approaches to both composing and performing, Feldman writes, "I added another link to the chain, and they called it freedom".[138] Susan Sontag is more explicit with regard to the dilemma Feldman identifies, and extends her focus to literature and to art generally. She writes that,

> Practiced in a world furnished with second-hand perceptions, and specifically confronted by the treachery of words, the artist's activity is cursed with mediacy. Art becomes the enemy of the artist, for it denies him the realization – the transcendence – he desires.[139]

"[D]o we love Music," Feldman asks, "and not the systems, the rituals, the symbols – the worldly, greedy gymnastics we substitute for it? That is, do we give *everything* – a total commitment to our own uniqueness?"[140] The answer is that we cannot. If we love music, then we love, in some part, the systems, rituals, and symbols through which it exists. A commitment to uniqueness can be perceived as such only via the greedy gymnastics by which our conceptions are organised. There is no transcendence. The challenges and possible solutions that are the stage for creativity in any given field are always already contaminated. Feldman is in fact resigned to this reality: he writes, "to make something is to constrain it. I have found no answer to this dilemma. My whole creative life is simply an attempt to adjust it".[141] Creators work within disciplines that allow, at best, renewed impressions of a purity that can never be reached. This is not the end of creativity, but the endless beginning. Contrived and relative renditions lead to more and other acts of persuasion. Creative redemption can be sought again and again. How, this chapter asks, are a poet's technical contracts involved in the impressions of significance for which redemption is (consolingly) pursued?

Considerable satisfaction can be generated by a poem that seems to fulfil the contract that informs it. Publication and the consequent physical presence of a poem in a public space might heighten the sense of achievement. Its author might conclude that the work has indeed reached a point where it withstands its impossibility (as Blanchot says it must). His or her experiences and impressions may seem to have been translated into compelling, poetic expression, and the relevance of both may seem to have been affirmed. A technical contract can at no stage guarantee such a result. Nor can it confirm its own fulfilment. Poets' perceptions of their works remain fundamentally insecure. Technical contracts are observable guides to the unobservable, affording a means of focus and of experimentation; they are also bearers of indeterminacy, being themselves founded essentially on contrivance. There are no right answers to the questions of which forms and techniques, or which rhymes and which rhythms, a poet should use. A devised contract may be substantially revised once a poem has been begun (as things "unobservable" come into play), demonstrating again that constraints and obstacles are such only by design. A poet is one who willingly commits to explicit artifice in order to approach a margin at which creativity can take place. This is the point of all technical contracts. The artifice offers no protection from the margin that is sought other than its own feigned specificity, as shaped by poetic traditions and by the preferences of the poet concerned. This can be enough. (Im)possibility can be particularised, uncertainty localised, and opportunities for creativity forged, as has been argued. The mediation Feldman laments offers a vital setting for creativity, a setting where there is neither absolute constraint nor an absence of constraint, neither automation nor incomprehension; unreadability can be glimpsed but need not overwhelm.

Contracts laced with the tension that is the freedom to conditionally choose are what permit and sustain creativity. Such contracts stage an expectation for certain *but ultimately unspecified* achievements. The creators employing them thus encounter both promise *and* uncertainty. Creative redemption arises from a creator's sense that his or her own influence has allowed the former to outweigh the latter: problems worth solving are ideally identified or constructed, and solutions are offered. Impossibility, to repeat, is to yield a mediated and compelling possibility. Can it be assumed here, and need it be assumed, that uncertainty and redemption are conscious concerns for a poet? Certainly, it is possible for poems to be written with relative ease: a poet need not be torn apart by angst each time he or she creates and may feel, on the contrary, largely confident with respect to the tools and processes employed. The occasional arrival of unexpected effects may be the only indication that a poet has approached any kind of Derridean threshold. The notion of creative redemption does not lose relevance in this scenario. Risks, in creativity, are inevitably taken. Comfortably or uncomfortably, a poet works without access to complete assurance, and his or her technical contracts, though they may offer direction and containment, nonetheless expose this reality. Amid openly concocted constraints and conditions, where expression is to be individual as well as conventional, a technical contract is a challenge to be met, and not a template for a satisfying work. Uncertainty need not be explicitly regarded by a poet, yet its presence will shape the experience. Without it, nothing is created.

In section I it was suggested that a poet does not choose uncertainty but, rather, responds to uncertainties that are always already available – these uncertainties can never be mastered or even fully encountered, yet there is a sense in which the poet becomes (as-if-)responsible for some small fraction of them. The notion provides an opportunity for an alternative description of the relations between uncertainty and poetic creativity. What might it mean, we can ask, for a poet to be responsible? The answer lies partly in another question: what is the difference, we can ask, between responsibility and oppression? While the latter centres on law and order, the former admits initiative amid law and chaos. Oppression celebrates determinateness, swallowing uncertainty prior to any creative act; responsibility celebrates meaning amid the threat of disorder, admitting a margin but also a way of and a will to not drown in its infusive spread. For Derrida, "an increase in responsibility" is *implied* by the relinquishment of an absolute centre.[142] Technical contracts reflect just such an increase. Care is taken by a "responsible" poet to relate an emerging, as-yet-chaotic poem to relatively stable points of reference. These points of reference may change, but will not be abandoned. The poet is thus revealed to be one who wishes both to remain a poet and to sustain the medium, even while he or she contributes works that do not wholly conform to established forms of poetry. The challenge of achieving redemption translates here into the difficulty that lies in deciding *how* to be responsible. "Frames, borders, constraints, and yet elasticity", writes John Kinsella; poems, he explains, "work through and against conventions, they are constantly grappling with responsibility and rebellion".[143] Even where the "rebellion" is not explicit, appearing as a relatively minor innovation within a largely conventional work, the struggle remains. Poets attempt to both perpetuate *and* renew poetic expression and risk failing one or the other ambition, or both, in doing so. This is the ridge to which their technical contracts ideally deliver them. It is in rescuing both ambitions, each from the threat of the other, change from preservation *and* preservation from change, that creative redemption is experienced. To accept responsibility in creativity is to lend the "*and*" importance.

Interlude: Irresponsibility

The easy poem, the writing that in writing slides just by saying the cloud in hot pursuit of this lady, shoulders over knees and
　　　gusting into the
　　　　　giraffes that range the treetops,
　　　　　most unbitten by what
　　　　　kind of fleeting bone
　　　　　toiling into mud, is
　　　　　the word, learning red, each dip
　　　　　like the horns between
　　　　　what the mutton wouldn't notice ++

Where does responsibility end and irresponsibility begin? It is possible to arrange loosely selected words in the shape of a poem without giving careful thought to their impact. Proponents of automatic writing might regard this positively. The resulting work may *look* poetic and could not be considered to have been written without any contract at all, but could it be said to have been written responsibly? How is it possible to say whether sufficient responsibility has been taken? To be pleased with an achieved effect is not necessarily to experience creative redemption. The question of whether the work is a poem must still be (subjectively) answered. Of course, the poet may not arrive at a clear yes or no; this, he or she might say, is the idea of a poem, just and not quite a poem.

sound

ti karrajun dis vyderon
mar deres le verifon
swi t'ka lahbillapor
ka kurrala
la Shisk;

kenanah shiss tukunanah
takun tahayn.

Conclusion

Mathematics, Motz and Weaver write, "is our intellectual telescope and microscope".[144] Michael Guillen describes it, equivalently, as "an exceptionally super-sensitive seeing-eye dog".[145] It is a seeing-eye dog with peculiar habits – there are some places it just will not go – yet this seems to improve its sensitivity within the locations it enjoys. Poetry is a telescope and a microscope for things non-mathematical. It, too, is an exceptionally super-sensitive seeing-eye dog with peculiar habits, and can act as such for poets as well as readers. The numerous, interactive constraints that form poets' technical contracts serve as tools for perceiving possibilities that would otherwise pass unnoticed. Like all good microscopes, they do not themselves explain what is detected. Multiple possibilities are also obscured by these tools, for the tools are necessarily biased. Creativity can at times be hindered. It is a point worthy of a digression. A commitment to a particular sound contract can "twist your thought," Richard Wilbur warns, and "take your mind off where you were going".[146] Wilbur adds:

> I think one could start out in a very difficult form, like terza rima, and find that the natural drift of the thoughts and perceptions was being impeded, was being falsified, by the technical difficulties. What you do at that point is to start over, maybe, or eliminate some of your rhymes.[147]

Technical difficulties can inspire a highly useful "drift of thought", one no less "natural" than that referred to by Wilbur. But they can also become a source of unproductive interference. A poet's liberating manacles can become just manacles, directives that, in the words of James Voss and Mary Means, "prohibit the individual from viewing problems in new ways".[148] "It is so easy," writes Miller Mair, "to get a new idea and destroy it by the old methods of approach that change and bend it".[149] It is difficult to know, of course, when a selected method might destroy an idea and when it might provide just the right support. A modern haiku poet must decide whether to embrace a strict syllable-count or, in accordance with current trends, to diverge from it: either choice might depress *or drive* his or her efforts. The point is not that certain forms and methods should be avoided, but that compliance for its own sake can smother creativity. A poet can detract from his or her experiences as a creator by directing attention *to* poetic forms and not, also, *through* them.

Technical contracts ideally offer form to ongoing processes of influence and exchange, processes creators undertake with both daring and responsibility. Like linguistic indeterminacies, poetic forms and techniques become a source of licence, effecting both freedom and constraint. There is no agreement here with Craig Raine's conclusion that, "Technique is something you learn in order to reach a point where you're writing what you want with the minimum of interference".[150] Rather, technique is what a poet learns in order to utilise and withstand what Blanchot, with characteristic exuberance, calls "the force of the undetermined". "The poet's destiny," Blanchot writes,

> is to expose himself to the force of the undetermined and to the pure violence of being from which nothing can be made, to endure this force courageously, but also to contain it by imposing upon it restraint and the perfection of a form. This is a requirement full of risk.[151]

Write by all means, Blanchot declares, "but only if writing always makes the act of writing more effortful".[152] There are no perfect forms, and the pure violence of being is not expressed. Yet technical contracts remain a means by which risks can be taken and new expressions tried. The force of the undetermined is not contained, yet ongoing creativity (and creative redemption) is perhaps in any case the more interesting ambition.

Intermission: Playing with Form

Blanchot suggests writers might let words become "gazes, an empty light, attractive and fascinating", such that "a new contract forms with things' intimacy, a presentiment of unknown relations".[153] The "empty light" is a compelling opportunity. An effect is to be found that will seem not only to fill the emptiness but to (temporarily) eclipse the potential for *other* intimacies. Such would be its persuasion. Words and sounds can be sufficient to engage the fascination Blanchot refers to. Line and stanza shapes can similarly shine their urgent possibilities. They can guarantee nothing. The forms, the sounds, the silences, and the revisions a poet entertains essentially deliver, in this way, both a location and a degree of doubt through and against which his or her creative powers can be directed. The doubt sensed, and the degree found to be useful, will be specific to individual poems and poets. Rewarding works will not be forced from simply any constraint at all and what is invigorating for one poet may seem awkward or false to another. But the allure, the pull towards creativity, the sacrifice of the gaze to the call for redemption, will accompany each opportunity that is found.

And what else? What then happens in the struggle to establish "a new contract …with things' intimacy"? Responsibility vies with rebellion. Forms might be stretched and revised. Or employed to support semantic or conceptual play. Cross-discipline influences might offer new creative material. Risk is constantly brought into balance with what it is that might be achieved. Constraints and liberations are equally exchanged, equally enjoyed, as the artist engages with his or her *indefinite* discipline, a discipline in which something *else* is always possible – this, again and again, is the key.

Postcard

    ° Felix turns air into living muscle – it's his own wild song
    and a near liberation. He stares at his own breath – the flock
    rises. And though storms and abrasion land transfigured wings,
    he's pleased – the new birds' travel stuns us all.

Six Wishes

1. the death of that desire
to have anything at all
while wanting nothing;

2. to feel the rush of what it takes to speak,
and then to not speak: the hover
where the writhing of those six or seven words
trickles into silence;

3. anything not yet marred
by what the eye might call
the mothering of the tongue

4. and that the mirror
has to bend to see –
the moment of revolution;

5. to voice the doubt in my own voice
but not believe;

6. to feed wheat threshings
to the romantics
in the back paddock –
not quite sacrificial.

Postcard

◦ John cuts the embroidery in the portrait of his life, staring into
stretched beige – he says there are patterns where the threads were,
and he's sure he's seen, through one of the holes, a distant light.

Doubt

    bees crawling (the
honey in the
    bones) without a queen.

Wait

fronds sprout from the seeds
in her porous bones.

Arrival

    disengaged, the mechanics of night
roll out into vistas.

Want

Trees in the bottom paddock,
hooking toes in the dark ground,
wrestle from unweathered soil,
to hurl through leaftips, the dry

too long unending; and wind,
revelling in the trees' throws,
looses in the tangling air
incantations of its own,

rends from the roots of mountains
ligatures of black cloud, steeped
still in shadow. The weight of
stone sifts through the sky's lungs and

leans on the trees' boughs, and yet
drops refuse to fall: ensnared
in the wind's yearning, the rain
swells, rolls, and the dry deepens.

(U l) t i m (a t) e l y

Zeus appears before you.
Do you mention it?

Trust takes its chances

Throw away the husk. As if the kernel might come after. My dad's
a paperbark. My mum's an oak from the other side of another country.
I'm an outline, a hybrid in a breeze, that wraps the whole unravelling,
seed right through to trunk. Throw it away? Throw it away!
    And if the kernel hasn't formed,

                                        ...search through the raging grass

A20

    there's a man in a car park leaning against a convertible to get a better
view of what other kind of life he might have led. It's night. There's glass on
the asphalt that lights like a torch beam searching into his soles each time a
car passes on the highway. He's half crouched, facing out, and it's a corner-
of-the-eye peer into the vacant back seat, which breathes, like an old lizard,
some couple, he thinks, still warm with fucking, digesting on its insides. He
climbs behind the wheel, breaking onto the outside of a town he's never
loved. Ignition whirs through his bones, and he's free, sliding from the car
park. The glass shards light up in his peripheral vision as he turns along the
highway. For a moment, choking, he's everyman, driving home... but
there's fire in his soles, and speeding, he
                                        leaves it all behind.

5109   14   + 948

Number Storm

644 198 + 5x   0.1   + 1

45 899 × 2334 + π − 66 778 126 775 667 − (27 ÷ 8.7) ÷ 9 762 722 × √(-2) × e + 7 − 1 628 336 437 638 823

7336 ≈ 66 020 < 34 × 7955 + 76 + 255   a bruise   653 34.776 + i × (6 + sin π) − 28/9 > 6 − 6688e

77 845 606 + 2^5 − 61   musters in the skull   7310.7892 + 5i = 7^x − 9i × sin (sin (sin 57x) + 8848 × x^{7y}

10^8 ÷ √87 × 0 + 27 > 1.38 − 3610 − 8723 + 70/3.4149 ÷ 56 × ((3 + 8x) + cos 3x) = (9y + 4) ÷ 78x

68 778 − 8.977 ÷ x/2 + (3x × 7949 × 3π/5 − 2π) − √46999 ÷ √(6 − √(39.42 × (e + πi)) + 95343/5) + 862582^6

3847 − 48110 × x + √5 − 1.45 ÷ 21 844 634 390 + 2   spreads   1993.67/√3 ÷ (288 ÷ π) + x^{3x+2} − 7 = 9y + 3

sin (x + 5.4e) × eπ × 0 + 915.6 + 12 × 8 + (sin $3x^3$ − 6(y^2 − 2y) × √(3x + 9)) − (7 − ($23x^2$ × (2 + 6117.3)))

391 × 6.24 × 81x   across the eyes   39 979 418 + 1234 + (178sin (3x + y) × 761) − 2 − 2^2 × ($73x$ × 873$)^7$

4728 ÷ 917 × (5 + $6x^9$) + cos 3x + 47955 × 399π + (5 − 4 + 77) × 23 × 5.266 + √5.267 − 3^{5x} − √(54/π − 7)

5 × 2 = 10x + 98.4 − (45sin ($7y^6$ ÷ 523.87 + (4 − 2y)) + 1) + 6/8 + 3.033   humidity   7546 ÷ √8x ÷ 3

2.773874 − 37^{2x} × 6e × 9/6.7 − (510 − (288y − ($6y^3$ − e))) ÷ 4 − 2 × 2/3 × 745 669 080 + 500 × 11.38 ÷ 1486

1 + (29 389 × 57/3) − 3π × 1007.644 + (22.542 + $36x^4$) ÷ π   rising   2665 − 3 + sin πx + (2664.779^2 × 3) × 9 510

503π × 89.37 × 6y + (2 ÷ √(e − π)) × √(7812.803 + $37y^2$)/5.01104 − 3   the sweat   6 × √(-5) × 0.8 ÷ π + 2

sin x ÷ 6861 × √(5x + $12x^4$) − 3.1009 + √(724 − 8133) + 9 × e − (1771.399058 × π) + 85 × 51/918 ÷ ($69y^2$ × √4)

6 ÷ π × (38 × 2π) ÷ 9 × √118   like a tease   (1009 − $2^{-3}$$)^2$ + 176^5 × 164 781 780 + sin y^2 = 6x + π

60 × (742/4 ÷ 8)   will it   √(-9 + 2.25x) + 610 × (71 − (x^{25} + 4/6) ÷ 3) − 900 030 220.01 × 610y × $3y^3$

44414.44 × $3e^3$ + (8 × 4) × 1 − 461 × 487π + (3y + 8y × (33x ÷ 5 + 883)) × 3 + 2 − (16x ÷ sin (8x + 9)) × 5

4627 × 32 006 920 446.000204 + $7^{3.8}$ × 12 197 080 023 + (sin 7.6x × 2π) + 35 300 × 69 + 855 555 9 ÷ cos y

isin x + 968 × √26.7 − √(6π − 8)   rain 4673^6 + x^2 + 65 × ((e + 4) × (π - 28.5)) × 68 340 ÷ (x − y)

64 048 003 + 774.19 − (5^x × $9x^3$) × 2137   will the   618.19782 + 3.28/7   storm $517x^{10}$ ÷ 3 × √(182 ÷ 7.9)

4.769 × i + x^x ÷ 92 − 8x/4 + 96 587.143 + (x^{y+4} + 5x − 8) × 1.9287 × (4 − cos y) × 0.0081 − 46t($10y^{18t}$ ÷ 5x)

break   √(89 − 5/12 + (x^4 − $3x^2$ + 9)) − √π ÷ 93 + (37.1976 + 5^{19}) − 46/105 + x^e ÷ 0.065 × √(56 − π × x^{368x}) + 49

60 814 × 60.83 − (37x ÷ 784/π + 43)   …here   565561 × (37π + 73x$)^3$ = 83 × (√8.9 + √(3 ÷ π))

3425227937 + 3 × (288.37 × sin π) + √8   in the weather's 567 8

7   hold 6 1

20 0   445

77

A Word from Mathematics

"A very common pitfall when using any kind of transform is to forget the presence of the analyzing function in the transformed field, which may lead to severe misinterpretations..." Marie Farge.

The analysing function
doesn't draw attention to itself   *to see*
                                                                        all
as being part, effectively,   *of a thing*
of the phenomena under study.

                                                                        we say
You can measure its impact, but for this
you need an analysing function,   *the all*
                                                                        lies
which won't draw attention to itself
as being part, effectively,   *elsewhere;*

of the function under study.
You can measure its impact, but for this   *a quiet*

you need an analysing function,   *deflection*
which won't draw attention to itself

as being

Algebra

so much depends
upon

a and b,
track marks

through figured
fields,

finding x in the
cool of y.

Postcards

○ Atoms in the in-breath swap electrons with particles from the
body's cells; Cass exhales and bits of her begin the journeys
she's always dreamed about.

○ Grace says it's a matter of kidding the mind into thinking there's
still some kind of order. Serge says she doesn't know what she's
talking about... So she must be right.

Milling

I grind with my own bones
the ink and white

fibres
and find no

secret hidden
between the words.

Pen
in hand.

The new page
empty. Trinkets fall:

loved
ones,

hunger,
sleep.

I find the husk
of

fortitude: "here",
the poem

feeds, "here
"you have written

"your name".

Section III: Appeal

Aesthetic Constraints

A poet's task is to draw the personal and the poetic to a significant intersection. Experiences and associations are to be cast persuasively into poetic forms and sounds. Failure, in the form of an unsatisfying work, is always a possibility. Compromise is inevitable. Success is inherently questionable. What, then, motivates the effort? Miller Mair, interpreting comments by the scientist Michael Polanyi, writes:

> Polanyi suggests that any inquiry not guided by intellectual passions would inevitably fan out and dissipate itself in endless trivia. Our sense of scientific beauty, he implies, helps us towards our vision of reality and also suggests the kinds of questions that may be reasonable and interesting to pursue.[154]

The mathematician, physicist, and philosopher, Henri Poincaré, too, suggests that creators make choices according to their "aesthetic sensibility". Arthur Koestler, in response to Poincaré, writes that the "useful combinations are precisely the most beautiful, I mean those best able to charm this special sensibility".[155] A creator may be dragged away from where his or her fancy has flourished by a desire to make an idea more accessible: beauty and passion may be compromised for certain practicalities. Yet aesthetic appeal is undoubtedly an intense force in creativity, in art more obviously (which is not to say more) than in science. What, then, are the personal and poetic needs and ideals that allow poetry to seem worth writing? What lends enthusiasm to a poet regarding his or her pursuit of a particular kind of poetry? And what is it that can commit a poet to an endeavour that is likely to be, in so many ways, a frustrating one? These are the concerns of the current section. James Voss and Mary Means conclude that it is "value" and "affect" that "drive the process" of creativity.[156] The interest here is in finding support for this assertion in the general practice of poets.

The claim to be submitted is that poets accept and negotiate aesthetic *contracts* just as they accept and negotiate *technical* contracts. The two are indeed inseparable: technical contracts are devised and employed according to their perceived potential to yield aesthetically pleasing poems and processes, and pleasing poems and processes are in part those that satisfy given technical contracts. The circuit, however, is not closed. Aesthetic contracts involve poets in broader and more complex concerns. In the following chapter, a description is offered of one of the most widely accepted aesthetic constraints poets encounter, namely the need to produce poems that are recognisably individual. In chapter three, a range of ideals are more generally considered, primarily to highlight the conditions and contexts through which a poet may decide whether a poem is aesthetically persuasive. Specific contexts may support and/or frustrate the ideals a poet embraces. Chapter four considers the relations between aesthetic contracts and uncertainty. By their nature, ideals carry considerable ambiguity. Not being grounded in actuality, wrapped up in the mystery of what it means to attain perfection, brushed with a sense of the mythic, ideals are what has not quite been grasped, both elusive and illusive. Their presence is in this sense haunted by absence, and the question becomes: is this an absence that can be creatively redeemed? If so, what is peculiar about the aesthetic elements of a poet's experiences of redemption? In the final chapter of section III, the focus shifts from the need for poets to perceive appeal in particular poems to the need for appeal to be perceived with regard to the overall act of creating. The intimate contracts that afford aesthetic appeal to poetry *as a vocation* are as much a part of the creation of poetry as any of the field's other supports and provocations. Aesthetic value, it is argued, is not a contract in poetry alone, but in thought and emotion generally. Creative redemption is a weak experience, and unlikely to be pursued, where the act of creating is not psychologically significant.

Interlude: Idealism

A poet's commitment to writing poems will be informed, in part, by the commitments of previous poets. By reading the celebrated works of earlier writers, a poet learns what has been possible in poetry. He or she may also begin to set the new challenge: to write those poems that will not only match (or surpass) all that has been achieved, but that will also capture what is peculiar to no other time and to no other writer.

To call ourselves modern

Voices from the unforgotten dead uncoil with whispers
Of what it means to roll the salts of mortal cells
Beyond mere flesh, to where scrawls from vanished hands
Infect the weather, to where words filtered by the mind
Bear covenants with the weight of rain, while the tongue
Passes with its speaker to an unheeded grave.

To call ourselves modern, we carve into trodden ground and dream
Our own arrival, our sun-demented storms, gold-edged and terrible.
We speak of winds, of rain clouds bent over glossy fields,
And of the murmurings of the remembered dead, who when storms
Break, will almost, *almost* drown. As if here we might renew ourselves –
The first streams, the first flood, loosing light in genesis.

Rage. Rage. And skyward. Hard lips and iron bones. A sliver of skin
Pressed between air and soil in the acid scent of passing.
We aspire. The hand still living stretches for the nets of cloud,
And there, folds its chrysalis into downpours. The voice still speaking
In its unforgotten urge, implants its threaded whispers. And the veins
Of time veer into a past thus transfigured. *Feel* the transfiguring!

So we would bloom. And so we would forge, in the hold of reverence,
A newer age. The quiet words. Waiting.

A Unique Repetition

Perhaps the most fundamental obstacle to be overcome in a poet's efforts to produce an aesthetically pleasing poem is the double bind that says past poems are to be emulated but not copied – the new is to equal (or surpass) the old *distinctively*. The best available guides as to what might work well in a poem are presented as the unavailable property of *other* poems. It is necessary, in other words, to produce comparable and recognisably poetic effects using details and forms that are agreeably new. "To conform merely," T.S. Eliot tells us, "would be for the new work not really to conform at all; it would not be new, and would therefore not be a work of art".[157] For Hart, describing essentially the same dilemma, a poem "cannot abstain from imitating other poems" – this "is its chance of life and its fear of death".[158] The difficulty translates into the intense question of how a poem fits against and survives in relation to the poems that precede and surround it. Imitation is vital if a work is to be recognised as poetry. Yet *inappropriate* imitation (and it need not be clear to a poet precisely what this entails) can destroy a poem's (and a poet's) credibility. To mimic too overtly or too excessively can be to imply either humour or deference, the second of which tends to be seen, in current western contexts at least, as a sign of weakness, if not as unethical. The unwritten contract, here, states that a persuasive poem is one that is in some regard *unique*. History is to be acknowledged but must also be extended, as proof of participation in the present. Is this, though, a matter of aesthetics, or merely a definition of creativity? The point to emphasise, in answer, is that it can be aesthetically displeasing in poetry to produce a poem in which one's individual, creative influence is not *acceptably* evident. Morton Feldman exclaims, more generally, "Art is a crucial, dangerous operation we perform on ourselves. Unless we take a chance, we die in art".[159] While it is not suggested here that a poet is required to evidence revolutionary originality, Feldman's comment does emphasise that there is more at stake than the production of something that is simply new. A chance must be taken. There are risks involved. Only certain operations will be successful. In poetry, an aesthetically pleasing poem is one that both swerves from and sustains poetic traditions in ways that accord with the values and experiences of those involved. Contracts are negotiated in relation to specific contexts and circumstances.

The tensions evoked by a creator's need to mimic without mimicry (so to speak) are discussed at length by Harold Bloom, who describes the anxiety involved as a "Sublime terror determined to maintain itself".[160] When poets create, their works enter a field already spectacularly inhabited. Mentors may inspire new effort. A.S. Ostriker, for example, describes Whitman as, for her, in her own writing, "killer of the censor and clearer of ground".[161] But Bloom acknowledges greater complexity. "There is no unmediated vision," Bloom writes, "whether in poetry or in any other mode, but only mediated revision, for which another name is anxiety, in the Freudian sense of 'anxious expectations'".[162] The young poet, in Bloom's description, becomes the struggling son of the oppressive poetic father. There is an intense, Oedipal agon, resolved only by the young poet's displacement or revision of the power of the older poet, who is loved and admired, but also hated and feared. Poetic creativity becomes, for Bloom, a process of mis-taking, mis-interpreting, or creatively correcting what has gone before. The young poet, Terry Eagleton explains, summarising Bloom's position, must "clear a space for his own imaginative originality".[163] The act is tempered by a form of regard, for there is hubris, a devastating arrogance, in a child who knowingly works towards the displacement of the parents he loves. Anxiety, here, would arise from the threat of failure, but also from the threat of success, for success would bring with it a devaluation of the informing works. If the child was in turn displaced, the logic of poetry, on which the poet depends, might also begin to decline. Impressions of the value of poetry might seem to be weakened; certainly, they would need to be revised. The poet would become something other than a poet in the traditional sense. Without such a revolution, creative redemption would reflect a dual resolution: the threats of failure and of success would be contained (tenuously) by a reverently irreverent poem, a poem, that is, that seemed both novel *and* poetic, embracing, to repeat, both rebellion *and* responsibility. "'Be me but not me' is the paradox of the precursor's implicit charge", Bloom explains.[164] Blanchot, too, offers that in order to produce a new work, a writer "must destroy language in its present form and create it in another form, denying books as he forms a book out of what other books are not".[165] The love of the parents and of the self merge in an entity that is not quite either.

Bloom tells us that only the uncommon "strong" poet battles successfully against the anxieties creativity induces. The battles are becoming, Bloom elaborates, increasingly difficult, for the young poet is in contest with an ever-greater number of heroic forebears. It is with these comments that Bloom's argument and the argument given here diverge. Poetic effects, it can be conceded, are not freely available. The limitation, however, need not be deemed a threat to a poet's imagination (as Bloom implies it is[166]), but as a constraint that both supports and provokes. Since a constraint is itself a kind of threat, and since the threat Bloom describes can act (for the strongest of poets) as a spur for creativity, the distinction needs to be clarified. The challenge offered by the "be me but not me" charge is to rob, fragment, and recombine selected materials while still producing works that feel both personal and poetic. In the act of writing, the risk of inappropriate imitation becomes a specific problem in need of novel solutions. The strong poet, Bloom suggests, is one who can endure the (ever-increasing) guilt that near-imitation entails. What is argued here is that guilt in creativity exists as one of many sources of uncertainty, and that this uncertainty has the potential to drive a creative response in any poet. The increase in the number of constraints (the effects that cannot be copied) is also an increase in the number of sites for creative endeavour. For current purposes, a "strong" poet would be one who experienced a sense that sufficient uncertainties had been both approached and answered in a poem, "sufficient" being a subjectively negotiated standard. There is no means by which the label of "strong" might be objectively applied, particularly not with reference to guilt alone. The "be me but not me" charge will undoubtedly establish a presence, but will not act in isolation. The context is broader than Bloom seems to allow.

Bloom does acknowledge the operation of uncertainties other than Oedipal anxiety. Opportunities for creativity, his comments imply, are delivered via linguistic indeterminacies: "Power is in the traversing of the black holes of rhetoric," he writes, "where the interpreter reads his own freedom to read".[167] But the gesture is restricted. Bloom allows that ambivalence and anxiety can drive the production of poetry, but describes the resulting poems as an ever more enfeebled retaliation against a smothering oppression.[168] For Bloom, Hart reflects, "the sublime moment of creativity is thoroughly negative, a perverse revenge on what enables it".[169] Bloom *almost* acknowledges a Derridean threshold. His emphasis, however, is not placed on a capacity to move continually between chaos and order (a capacity that is, for Derrida, joyous), but on Oedipal rivalry in the move from one sense of order to another, a move increasingly disabled by the "blight" of belatedness.[170] Freud teaches us, Bloom insists, "that our most authentic moments tend to be those of negation, contraction and repression".[171] "To defend poetry," Bloom adds, "which is to say, to defend trope, in my judgment is to defend defense itself".[172] Yet creativity is also about delight, affirmation, and exploration, which is not to say that these qualities cannot involve defences of numerous kinds, but that they can also and *equally* involve acts of discovery and revelation. There is much still on offer, for the domain of poetry is not a closed world but a changing conglomeration of multiple, interactive influences, technical and aesthetic, poetic and non-poetic, institutional and circumstantial. The "be me but not me" charge, as an aesthetic constraint, is a resource and an opportunity. At once directive and ambiguous, the charge becomes a tool for approaching new possibilities, an observable guide to the unobservable, operating amid a complex web of such constraints. The threat and difficulty it poses to individual creators can be viewed as part of the challenge of and scope for creative persuasion. If the charge is limiting (it can be frustrating, for example, to wish to use a word or technique that the success of another poem has rendered unavailable), it is at once an invitation for the poet to enter another kind of poetic space, one more specific to the new circumstances, and in this there can be significant reward.

Interlude: Be Me But Not Me

"Tenacity" is a tiff fought with the poetry of e.e. cummings. cummings' distinctive use of punctuation, word fragmentation, and "erroneous" capitalisation lends his poems (for readers who are familiar with them) a strong presence in any works that employ even vaguely similar techniques. The struggle to repossess these techniques is essentially doomed. *Do something else*, the poets cry. *Alternatively*, a poet may offer an openly influenced, happily participating poem, impudently seeking forgiveness in the name of what is achieved (uniquely) within the mimicry.

Tenacity:

a buried
       s e a
that when oNe
  dRop
(in darkness)
  i m a g i n e s
     the briE(e)fest
light,
      grips,
tow
ing
  each
dam
        n (!) joint
   through the
s T ee l
  oF
     (fr o m t
     h e he ar
     t i ts elf)
  an
   o ut
flowing
    tide.

Contextual Idealism

Aesthetic contracts emerge, broadly, as ideals and aspirations, of which the "be me but not me" charge is one. More intimate examples can be given. Shelley's *Defence of Poetry* describes a preference for poetry that "lifts the veil from the hidden beauty of the world, and makes familiar objects be as if they were not familiar".[173] The bias is echoed in Shklovsky's claim, quoted earlier, that the "technique of art is to make objects 'unfamiliar'".[174] A further and widely shared ideal is given voice by Yves Bonnefoy when he claims that, "poetry is an experience of what goes beyond words".[175] Charles Wright, lending depth to the super-sensitive, seeing-eye-dog theory, offers an analogy: "It's best to keep unwritten as much as possible. Poetry is just the shadow of the dog. It helps us know the dog is around, but it's not the dog. The dog is elsewhere, and constantly on the move".[176] In the famous opening line of Stevens' "Man Carrying Thing" we are told, also, that "The poem must resist the intelligence / Almost successfully".[177] It is an ideal illustrated in many of Stevens' poems: in the lines, "The palm at the end of the mind", "an insolid billowing of the solid", and "the ear is glass, in which the noises pelt",[178] impossible images rub against an offer of import; a sustained contradiction is induced, an amphibian between the unreal and the real, between the insensible and the sensible, that teases the possibility of direct knowledge. In Forbes' work, effects that "resist the intelligence" are noted by Alan Wearne: "Reading a Forbes poem," Wearne suggests, "is like whitewatering, or abseiling. You just leap off and hope the poem holds".[179] The risks these writers take (the risk of incoherency, for example) are shaped and contained by the aesthetic contracts each bears in mind. Theodore Roethke is under no obligation to explain how "pure despair" can be represented as "My shadow pinned against a sweating wall".[180] Nor need cummings formally resolve his "eyes which are really petals".[181] The lack of obligation regarding strict elucidation is a mark of freedom, but *also* of a commitment to a constraining ideal. An aesthetic contract, like its technical counterpart, liberates as it manacles.

In what contexts do aesthetic constraints operate? Fred D'Aguiar describes poetry as "that art of the marvellous, of a simultaneous compression of language and an endless expansion of meaning".[182] The endless expansion, like the moving shadow of an unwritten dog, and like Stevens' resisted intelligence, serves as the aesthetic partner to selected technical structures (for D'Aguiar, among other things, a "compression of language"). Each lends persuasion to the other. Partnerships between poetic forms and ideals can be highly distinctive, characterising, for example, a poet's work, a genre, or an era of poetry. What is appealing with respect to one partnership need not seem so in other settings. The contrasts between haiku and limericks provide an example – what is desirable or daring in one is very likely to seem unsatisfying in the other. What is licensed in one era, similarly, may seem unattractive at other times. Referring to the work of James McMichael and Frank Bidart, Alan Williamson observes a tendency "to end lines on words like 'of', 'there', and 'or'". Williamson writes: "For any previous generation, such enjambments would have been a sign of weakness or lack of skill; for this one, they seem the sign of impetus and intensity, of an exacting quest".[183]

Aesthetic contracts are born in response to existing poems, to the available opportunities for writing, and to developments in other domains, as well as to a poet's particular partialities. "Creativity," Paul Magnuson concludes (in a discussion of Coleridge's "Fears in Solitude"), "is often a collaboration in conflict and confusion rather than a tranquil meditation of the individual mind".[184] Poets write, further, amid experiences that are not merely perceived by them but through which they perceive. Hence, Ramazani suggests we should turn to the modern elegy,

> expecting not so much solace as fractured speech, not so much answers as memorable puzzlings. Anything simpler or easier would betray the moral doubts, metaphysical skepticisms, and emotional tangles that beset the modern experience of mourning and of self-conscious efforts to render it. We need elegies that, while imbued with grief, can hold up to the acid suspicions of our moment.[185]

Marjorie Perloff acknowledges a more specific exchange: conflict and confusion in the relations between poetry and the media, she implies, has amplified various post-modern tendencies in the former. The need to produce something distinctively poetic amid the abundance of striking visual effects and symbolism provided by the media has encouraged, Perloff suggests, a "suspicion of 'imagefull' language".[186] Poetry has responded not just to the media but to (and inseparably) the technologies available for dissemination. Influences arising from the tools and materials for writing are by no means new. Félix Guattari has argued that machines can invite and, via the cultural assemblages in which they appear, even impel, with or without resistance, certain kinds of undertakings.[187] In Old English poetry, the "machine" was a severe material limitation: poems were written on valuable vellum no part of which was to be left bare.[188] Numerous poetic effects could not afford to seem appealing under such conditions, though others (including the expressive use of colour) took their place.

The external influences through which poets' aesthetic contracts are inevitably formed can at times become oppressively restrictive. The ideals promoted by strong, political regimes carry this potential. For the Russian poet, Marina Tsvetaeva (1892-1941), opposition to increasing socialist powers prompted self-exile.[189] The German Jewish poet and dramatist, Nelly Sachs (1891-1970), also sought escape from what was for her a threatening regime; the ruling bias in the country of her birth yielded no place either for her work or for herself.[190] A milder oppression, an inversion of Tsvetaeva's and Sachs' exiles, is described by Laurie Duggan. There was a time in Australia, Duggan perceives, when getting published was virtually impossible if you happened to be an Australian who had not been accepted *elsewhere*. Duggan suggests of himself, John Forbes and John Tranter, that, "we were probably the first literary 'generation' for whom it wasn't vital to go overseas (it was interesting and worthwhile even, but not vital)".[191] A poet, of course, can also inflict oppression on him- or herself. Philip Larkin states, for example, that it is "fatal to decide, intellectually, what good poetry is because you are then in honour bound to try to write it, instead of the poems that only you can write".[192] An aesthetic contract, the comment implies, can become, rather than an observable guide to the unobservable, a self-conscious doctrine upheld for its own sake. Responsibility can be lost to obedience.

Aesthetic contracts are functions of particular times, places, poets, and poetic forms. Each contract will reflect a poet's understanding of what poetic creativity ideally entails, both in relation to poetry (past and future) and the surrounding culture. Where this understanding exposes strong contradictions (between, for example, what a poet would like to write and what is described, by law, as allowable), creativity can be impeded. Yet the opposite extreme, a lack of contradiction, the seamless achievement of an apparently incontestable ideal, would seem to be no more conducive to creativity. A collaboration in conflict and confusion, a multiple spread of influences and commitments, imprecise ambitions: these are the sources of uncertainty that act as sites and spurs for creative redemption. What can be done here, the poet asks, full of force and desire; what needs to be overcome to give shape to what is beautiful?

Interlude: Incontestability

From the time of Euclid (third century BC) until the 1800s, Euclidean geometry had been the only and, for most, the true and natural geometry, "exact, eternal, and knowable with certainty by the human mind".[193] The arrival of non-Euclidean geometry was initially resisted.[194] Its eventual inclusion, effected partly by Einstein's use of non-Euclidean mathematics in his general theory of relativity, influenced not only mathematicians and physicists, but also creators in other fields. "For certain artists in the early twentieth century," L.D. Henderson reports, "non-Euclidean geometry was to be synonymous with the rejection of tradition and even with revolution".[195] Yet Euclidean geometry remains dominant in general thought – in basic schooling, it is the only geometry that is taught. Reuben Hersh insists that physics "gives no license to favor Euclid over non-Euclid".[196] Yet with Davis and Marchisotto, Hersh reports that, "Even now, it seems that most educated people believe in the Euclid myth".[197]

Losing the Dream
(or, Riemann's opus shuffles by)

We remain at home.
No-one's surfing into solar winds.

Vision loses sight to memory
like Pavlov's dogs.

We measure spheres in cubic metres,
straight lines on a rippling earth.

Across the cosmos, light
swerves on the contours of time's

involutions, and nothing is flat.
But we keep

to the common square,
arcs pinned onto level planes.

We stay as we are. There are hints
of a clandestine knowledge

we're told we cannot reach,
the sinuous music of a half-

forgotten tribe, where the heretics
work through a shadowed lens.

Riemann, Lobachevsky, Bolyai
shuffling by

while the safety
of local minds reigns.

We do not fly.

Redeeming Taste

Aesthetic and technical contracts do not impact on creativity in entirely comparable ways. Both contribute to the processes by which creators decide what promising problems look like and when responses to them are satisfying. Both offer a means of engaging concentration and of focusing creative effort, and both can disrupt that effort by embodying, or seeming to embody, potentially oppressive directives – obedience can seem to be required as the overwhelming response. They are both essential in some form if opportunities for meaningful creativity are to be pursued. Denying this last necessity in relation to musical creativity, and contradicting his own stated and previously quoted sense of entrapment (through mediacy), Feldman insists that,

> For ten years of my life I worked in an environment committed to neither the past nor the future. We worked, that is to say, not knowing where what we did belonged, or whether it belonged anywhere at all. What we did was not in protest against the past. To rebel against history is still to be part of it. We were simply not concerned with historical processes. We were concerned with sound itself. And sound does not know its history.[198]

The comment raises the first point of divergence between aesthetic and technical concerns. Feldman's works are recognisable as musical compositions; they were not composed in isolation from the field to which they do undoubtedly belong. What, then, is Feldman attempting to describe? Aesthetic contracts are devised in relation to specific contexts, yet in the subjective negotiations by which creators fashion their own versions or revisions of the ideals that are available, there are indefinitely many degrees of freedom. For a writer facing execution for anti-Establishment sentiments, this is no consolation. His or her predicament does illustrate, however, that even in strong regimes, there is room (with the risk of punishment) for individual choice. This freedom, this scope for individual daring, is the subject of Feldman's words. What the composer refuses to acknowledge is that such freedom requires a setting: it cannot be discerned, nor can anything seem significant, in an environment where there is no past or future. The differences between the freedoms technical and aesthetic contracts deliver can be used to partly explain Feldman's position.

Aesthetic contracts are not explicitly devices for creativity. They are infused with creative tensions but in ways more profound and more complex than for technical constraints. Considerable continuity with personal and non-poetic values is likely. Feldman's claim that he was "simply not concerned with historical processes" reflects this continuity. His own new notation had allowed significant deviation from dominant musical forms. Support for the application of this notation lay, it would seem, in values and ideals that through their emphasis on what was original, successfully "covered up" the necessary relations to existing practices, relations without which Feldman's work would not have been simply new but, rather, entirely other. The example is neither unusual nor entirely lamentable. An ideal that functions in this way, one that is selective in its vision, one that is essentially, and for its own sake, propagandist, may still generate considerable excitement and absorption, qualities that are enviable in creators of any kind. The gesturing by all ideals towards that hover of ambiguity known as absolute perfection, absolute purity, may well encourage such sleights of hand – it is tempting, perhaps, if also unjust, to lend a little transcendence to one's own ideas of what is good. Aspirations, positioned as they are above the shifting actualities of the day to day, will exist to some extent as articles of faith. This is the point. Belief, hope, and other emotional involvements inhabit, and often *deeply* inhabit, a poet's aesthetic contracts. And yes, this creates a potential for strong bias, but the trade-off is significant. Bias, effectively a constraint, liberates a creator's focus within a more specific field. An ideal held to be incontestable may even achieve such ends. While many opportunities for creativity will be removed by such insistence, others may be highlighted, and highlighted with sufficient force to inspire commitment, strong ambition, and highly concentrated creative work. The balance is delicate. Belief and emotional dedication may blind *and* inspire. They may also themselves become the subjects of revolution. Significant revision, a sudden revelation, an enlightening encounter – such change can inject considerable energy into a creative act. Beliefs and emotions do not come without risks. Conflict is not uncommon. What is once held as true may later be seen, or may be judged by others to be untrue or foolish. But the alternative, to hold no strong beliefs at all, can give rise to only a limited form of writing. An aesthetic contract is a description of that part of a poet's commitment to poetry that engages his or her sensibilities. Without this emotional involvement, a poem is an exercise in technique alone.

The charge of "be me but not me", the aesthetic constraint discussed in the second chapter of this section, calls for personal involvement by refusing to tell a creator *how* to repeat without repeating. The charge directs but also provokes; the poet who accepts the aspiration is met by uncertainty and so arrives at a site for creativity, wanting to respond. Many aesthetic constraints will operate in this way. Charles Wright's request to "keep unwritten as much as possible", to write "just the shadow of the dog", has inspired many writers partly *because* it cannot itself decide what is to be said and what is not. The constraint is tight and also indeterminate, a Stravinskian obstacle. To become emotionally committed to such constraints is to gain something to be redeemed *and* something worth redeeming. Yet not all elements of aesthetic contracts are hereby described. Larger elements, aesthetic preferences that are deeply cultural or psychological, perhaps even biological, are also part of the creative scene. These are influences that will not necessarily be available for interpretation, creative or otherwise. We are, Miller Mair writes, "inhabited by stories we know by and do not know about".[199] A range of creative possibilities may never be entertained by a creator, not because there is oppression, as such, but because they exist within assumptions he or she is not aware of or has never thought to question. There is also the element of affirmation. Any single creative act will affirm many more beliefs than it revises, the poet's blind assumptions among them. A creative act may indeed be pursued partly for this reason. An aesthetic contract can in this sense serve as a source of reassurance. This is reflected in the tendency for many poets to develop, wilfully or not, characteristic interests and styles. It is a tendency particularly visible among highly original poets. Emily Dickinson's poetry, for example, like cummings' poetry, is at once distinctive and repetitive, as if persuasion requires, and perhaps it does, the insistent claim that "yes, this effect is intentional" and "yes, I like it enough to do it again, and again, and again". "Be me but not me" is evidently a charge poets need not apply with equal force to themselves as to other poets. These observations reveal a relaxation of creative potential – unseen assumptions and insistent repetition close rather than open opportunities for creativity. They also suggest, however, that consistency and repetition are part of what allows specific expressions to seem convincing. Sufficient repetition (judged subjectively, where too much dulls creativity and where too little renders it superficial) can lend a sense of integrity both to a poet's poems and, for the poet concerned, to the endeavours that produce them.

Interlude: Uncertain Aspirations

To know how a haiku is technically defined but to have read very few of them is to allow the production of poems that may indeed contain five syllables in their first and last lines and seven in their middle line, but that do not respond to the aesthetic potential of the form, a potential developed over many centuries and interpreted, now, by poets both within and outside the original tradition. By reading and writing haiku, a poet may begin to acquire more complex ambitions, ambitions that are an urge for participation in certain ideals and values, and in the creativity they embrace. The basic technical contract of the haiku form might begin to be regarded more flexibly so that the needs of the developing aesthetic constraints might also be met. The resulting poems are likely to seem both more personal *and* more poetic.

from the suite, **Journeying**

to tilt
the evening light
the scrawny wings

flexing, sinuous,
they tilt the light fantastic
from recurring wings.

(ORIGINAL VERSION)

internet

no-one flies using feathers any more; each bird thinks of a destination and then
waits (birds along the wires,

queuing).

The Vocation of Poetry

Poets presumably, in some sense, *want* to subject themselves to the awkward demands of their discipline. Reward may lie in the end product, a work that is, ideally, technically sound, aesthetically appealing, and thematically compelling. Such rewards, however, are available to readers of poetry as well as to poets. For an individual to feel motivated to write, appeal needs also, and perhaps primarily, to be found in creativity itself. The attraction may reside in the sense of transformation: non-poetic materials become poetic, inklings become working images, constraining problems become unforeseen solutions, and so on. An opportunity, an absence, is framed, and the urge to test one's own and poetry's powers against it, the urge for creative redemption, can become its own source of energy. The act of writing might also offer the potential for a degree of concentration and absorption that is itself enjoyable. Unrelated tensions or boredom might be relieved in the process. Participation in a recognised community, the chance to identify or affirm personal abilities and beliefs, feelings of hope for particular poems, and a sense of risk, these, too, can contribute to a poet's desire to write. Such motivations must exist not only with sufficient force to compete with the many other actual and potential occupations in a poet's life, but with sufficient allure to render the accompanying sources of discomfort manageable. Discomfort is likely, in one form or another. Failure can be perceived as readily as success, disheartenment can oscillate with optimism, and much may need to be given up to make room for the act of writing. Perseverance requires that a poet can validate the pleasure and pain he or she encounters. What kind of pleasure will give what kind of meaning to how much unpleasantness (and perhaps vice versa) are questions poets implicitly and sometimes explicitly ask.

The concern of this chapter lies with those personal and complex contracts that afford aesthetic appeal to poetry as a vocation. In what sense can a poet's organisations of pleasure and pain be described as contracts, and how do these contracts differ from those relating to the appeal of particular poems? Vocational contracts can be described as those agreements, at once disciplinary and individual, by which poets render poetic creativity attractive and feasible. In practice, vocational appeal is experienced intermittently. Gratification is pursued not freely but where and if each act of writing allows. The implicit promise (always in doubt) is that any sacrifice of pleasure or desire will be balanced by sufficient reward. A poet might persist with a frustrating poem for days at a time, and over many months, with little to suggest that creative redemption might be imminent. Only the sense of the broader contract he or she has embraced can sustain the endeavour – the effort involved becomes valuable, perhaps even necessary, as part of a larger commitment. It is not suggested here that the agreement will be a plainly visible one, or that it is ever, or ever could be, formalised. What pleasure and pain are is a question individual poets may not themselves be able to fully answer. Eagleton, summarising Freud, writes, "our drives are in contradiction with one another, our faculties in a state of permanent warfare, our fulfilments fleeting and tainted".[200] Concord may be experienced as well as contradiction, and there may be moments of apparent peace as well as war, but at the very least, there is convolution. Pain can be pleasurable and pleasure painful, and both can be confused by external events and conditions. Multiple variables (from the light in a room to a family argument, from tiredness or illness to a political report or news from a publisher, from a friend's comment to the weather) can contribute to the sense that something promising (or not) has been undertaken. A creator creates partly because he or she is able, in the shuffle and deal, to regard and respond to pleasure and pain in ways conducive to creativity. What these ways are will depend on the individual and the circumstances involved. No attempt is made here to resolve the (irresolvable) complexities that are a poet's motivation. Much, though, can still be said.

There are certain kinds of experiences that poets need to be able to validate. It needs to seem appealing or endurable, for example, to spend concentrated time in conditions suitable for writing, despite the physical discomfort and isolation this can induce. It needs to seem appealing or endurable, also, to submit selected subjects or whims to a poetic bias. Donald Justice complains that, "the conception of a poem does usually in some respect seem more impressive, grander, than the finished product, which almost always represents a series of compromises between desire and necessity".[201] These compromises, which may derive from aesthetic as well as technical concerns, can cause a poem to diverge from the events, ideas, and feelings with which it began. Referring to an inceptive idea that could no longer be accommodated, Justice writes,

> I regretted its absence severely: a dimension of the poem was gone. But with the mild and familiar despair which accompanied this realization came also the hope that if such ironies had been necessary to the poem I had had in mind, they were probably not necessary to the poem I had very nearly written.[202]

Loss and despair are inflicted, here, by a constraint Justice willingly accepts, that of producing an effective poem. The pain is compensated for not only by the pleasure of a more promising work, but also by its *familiarity* as an element of creativity (Justice calls it a "*familiar* despair"). Here, as in the creation of any poem, the compromises poetic creativity entails acquire legitimacy in relation to the poetic bias to which commitment has been given. Loss and despair are balanced against notions of the poem's progress.

Experiences of doubt and uncertainty in poetic creativity need to be vindicated on many levels, not just in relation to the experiences that inform a poem. Benack, Basseches, and Swan, in their broad study of creative thinking, describe a need to develop epistemological beliefs that, while guiding specific problem-finding and problem-solving efforts, also tell us "how to feel about events in our mental life, such as discovering contradictions to our beliefs, being uncertain, or finding our beliefs changing".[203] Colin Martindale, in the same publication, writes that, "As the poet Samuel Taylor Coleridge long ago noted, creativity requires the ability to 'exist in ambiguity' or to *tolerate* disorder".[204] It requires, more precisely, the ability *not* to believe that one will exist in ambiguity *indefinitely*; disorder is tolerated, and perhaps actively sought, amid the tenuously arrogant belief that one's own powers will renew a satisfying sense of significance. A poet can be sustained in his or her work by the hope, or the need to show, that he or she is capable of arresting the threatened slide into irrelevance. Uncertainty is debilitating if it fails to be interwoven with this ambition. It merely confuses, that is, if no relation to opportunities for yielding persuasive poetic expression can be imagined. Such relations have been offered, formally and informally, by a number of writers. Keats's notion of negative capability, for example, broadly identifies an intimate relationship between uncertainty and the processes of writing. Described by Keats as "when a man is capable of being in uncertainties, mysteries, doubts, without any irritable reaching after fact and reason",[205] the notion itself offers a justification for entertaining the imaginative freedoms it refers to. Uncertainties, mysteries, and doubts are given a designated and promising significance as a vital part of a valued undertaking. In Blanchot's *The Space of Literature*, relations between uncertainty and creativity are secured by the word "inspiration", given optimistically to that which draws writers (impossibly) "into a space where truth lacks, where limits have disappeared, where we are delivered to the immeasurable".[206] Writers write, Blanchot explains, "by escaping the omnipotence of inspiration".[207] Again, the words establish a setting (and an accompanying enthusiasm) in which it is not merely good or understandable but remarkable to respond with hope to the indeterminacies that render creativity possible. Creative redemption, of course, is also an idea that attempts to situate uncertainty. All three conceptual structures defend a potentially dangerous dialogue with things chaotic. Indeterminacy is applauded. On a grander scale, Nietzsche offers us Zarathustra, the overman, who could, in Eagleton's words, "dance without certainties on the brink of the abyss. For him, the very groundlessness of the world had become a source of aesthetic delight and an opportunity for self-invention".[208] It is an exquisite vision, an extreme and energetic dream.

The kind and degree of uncertainty perceived as able to be entertained, like the kind and degree of pain perceived as endurable, will be specific to individual poets and to the poems they are writing. Greater uncertainty need not yield greater poetry. As ever, the influences and responses involved can be understood only in relative and circumstantial terms. The beliefs and experiences a poet works with are obvious variants. Voss and Means, referring to creativity in the social sciences, judge that, "One of the most critical components of mental functioning in general and problem solving in particular is prior knowledge".[209] As "prior knowledge", they include not just ideas about the work that tends to be done in a given field but also notions regarding the strategies people employ and the joys and hardships they experience. In poetry, the examples generations of poets provide can suggest the kind of effort or daring it might take to produce a satisfying work. What a poet knows and assumes about poets and poetry can accordingly be expected to impact on his or her relations to uncertainty. Such guidance, however, is double-edged. A poet who accepts, through others' examples, that certain experiences of and responses to uncertainty are possible and desirable *also* accepts the risk that such responses may not be possible for him or her specifically, at least not to the desired degree. Prior knowledge facilitates optimism and ambition, but also potentially threatening comparisons. Answers to the questions "To what might I contribute?" and "How might I do so?" can be followed by the questions "How am I faring?" and "Am I who I hoped I was?". Personal doubts may cause certain levels of uncertainty to be avoided, or may simply intensify the uncertainties that are experienced. A sense of self may be added to the list of things to be redeemed, or may be moved (since it is likely to be on the list already) to a higher, more prominent position. Blanchot is again informative. "Poetry", he states,

is only an exercise, but this exercise is the mind, the mind's purity, the pure point at which consciousness – that empty power to exchange itself for everything – becomes a real power, enclosing its infinite number of constructs and the whole range of its manoeuvres within strict limits. Art now has a goal, and this goal is the mind's mastery.[210]

A poet learns, in writing, that he or she has a mind with the force to write just the poem that is written. "From the poem the poet is born", Blanchot offers.[211] Uncertainty is pursued and responded to in the hope that there will be poems where the mind seems to approach its idealised potential, as conceived in relation to others' achievements *and* in relation to the particular ambition and self-belief (or self-hope) of the creator concerned. Amid constraints and absences, and surrounded by celebrated works, the task is to find a moment of strength, a moment that need never arrive to the satisfaction of its author and which can consequently lend to creativity both desire and dread. The risks are substantial – a poet's sense of, or desires for, his or her intelligence, skill, and sensibility are not protected from significant disappointment. A vocational contract is the balance of motivations able to tell such a poet that the risks are worth taking, maybe, even, that they *must* be taken.

Perhaps unsurprisingly, a capacity for creativity has been loosely associated with a tendency to perceive and suffer from uncertainties in everyday life. The list of famous creators described as displaying neurotic or psychotic behaviours is disproportionately long, crossing all fields and times, from Van Gogh to Cantor, Copernicus to Pollock, Elgar to Poe, and Handel to Hemingway.[212] Joyce Vantassel-Baska reports that, "Like Woolf and Bronte, Atwood viewed the art of writing as a triumph over neurosis".[213] It needs to be acknowledged that poets' organisations of pleasure and pain may have as much to do with their particular constitutions as with their experiences in poetry. Certain biological and biographical conditions may increase the likelihood that an individual will find allure in creative undertakings. Creative processes may seem, perhaps, to lend meaning and purpose to existing tendencies. A creator need not be mentally ill in order to create, nor need mental illness imply creativity. A creative discipline may seem, however, to offer licence to or a defence of, it may also exaggerate, a certain range of behaviours. No creative undertaking can be cleanly divorced from an individual's psychological state. *Any* individual, regardless of his or her mental health, can attempt to release personal tensions and disprove personal inadequacies (perceived or feared) by creating something new. Redemption can be sought for any doubted self. It is simply possible that the need for such enactments may tend to become more intense and more insistently sustained where certain kinds of instabilities already exist.

It is also true that doubt and uncertainty in everyday life can provide a creator with subjects conducive to creative work, subjects that, aside from being personal, offer ambiguities or difficulties that seem to demand a response. Nagging confusions can encourage creativity regardless of their source, and may attract greater concentration for being immediate concerns. The successful transferral of personal materials into the domain of an emerging poem may bring with it considerable relief. A sense of escape (from the personal to the poetic) and of, regarding the materials used, compensatory functionality (where unpleasantness becomes a resource) may add to a poet's commitment to the poem being written. Virginia Woolf writes, of her own experience, "Observe my own despondence. By that means it becomes serviceable. Or so I hope".[214] Many of Sylvia Plath's poems also read as examples of the "serviceability" to which Woolf refers. Poems written in these ways need not always be autobiographical. Personal discomposure can directly contribute to a poem, it may offer material with which to begin a poem, but need not be sustained as the poem's ultimate theme. Other associations and images may lead the poem to other ends. The same can be said, of course, for any marked and immediate feeling. Joy, awe, and revelation may also inspire creativity, and can elicit strong concentration without necessarily rendering the resulting poems diaristic. There is no argument, here, for the superiority of any theme or starting point for a poem. Trade with despondency is quite obviously not an absolute prerequisite for creativity. It does not answer the question of "How does a poet write well?", but only, and partially, that of "Why do some poems get written?".

Miller Mair, commenting on creativity, writes:

> Whatever evidence there is will seldom be enough to justify the steps we have to take beyond the known limits of our world. It is of the essence of this realm that we must sustain ourselves, or be sustained by the trust and relevant care of others, rather than protect ourselves from foolishness by the hard pellets of shared convention, tradable truths.[215]

It is not clear how Mair might distinguish between "trust and relevant care" and "shared convention, tradable truths". Each involves the other. Mair's gesture, however, would seem to be towards an acceptance of risk and uncertainty *provided* there is a context that lends sufficient meaning and hope to these otherwise unmanageable tensions. In poetry, some trust and some relevant care are broadly implied by the existence of the medium: the writing of poetry is a recognised and, in many ways, a celebrated occupation. A poet's vocational contract loses significant force without this foundation. Trust and relevant care are then extended by a poet's own organisations of his or her pleasure and pain, established relative to the knowledge of the discipline he or she possesses at the time. Value and purpose are lent to behaviours that ideally lead to creativity. Tensions can be induced, as when immediate pleasure is postponed for the sake of an unknown and potentially inadequate return, but the tension remains part of a larger order. A poet submits his or her impressions and hopes to uncertainties rendered approachable by the multiple constraints that inform this order. To be able to approach specific uncertainties is, in turn, to increase the need for redemption. A vocational contract directs and sustains what the poet hopes will be a rewarded effort. Assurance and predictability in this scenario can never hold force. Were they to, or were they to be seen to, opportunities for creativity would cease to exist – uncertainty would be given no location at which it might seem both interesting and accessible. The trust and relevant care a poet perceives and constructs are (like responsibility) the enabling substitutes for certainty. They are suitable associates for the doubt and risk that are to be entertained.

Interlude: Aesthetic Development

A poet's sense that his or her skills and tastes in poetry have improved can heighten an experience of redemption. The celebration is mixed, for it can entail, at once, the rejection of previously rewarding achievements. The possibility that currently pleasing poems will also fall out of favour inserts a new source of uncertainty, the drive then being to produce works that will endure. "If ardour prospers" redeems its former versions (written over several years), these having been rendered unconvincing by changes in the technical and aesthetic knowledge and bias of their author. The poem that redeems "If ardour prospers" is a possibility for the years ahead.

If ardour prospers

A hundred
thousand years
of human minds

and you
nestled in the timeline
like mist
in the rising sun.

You strive
against the glare,
surprised to learn

how in the wrinkles
of your small
hours,
the dew

whistles you
into love.

"Brief Appearance", PRECURSOR TO "IF ARDOUR PROSPERS"

A hundred thousand years of human minds,
hosted by the body;

and your own view, nestled in the timeline,
not quite as real, by your own account,

as the rising sun.
Plying your human form, you

strive against the glare, to learn
if ardour prospers.

A Moment Glistening, PRECURSOR TO "BRIEF APPEARANCE"

What he knew, each swirl,
Staged a border, a crest, a curving lip,
That would not be held –
He spoke,
And fed his sense to an older ocean,
Of drift and violent roll,
A hundred thousand years of human minds,
Of awe, and urge, and vision.

What he knew
Lived,
And passed,
Unpinned,
Though with an air, a flow,
Unbroken;
His view, his liquid thread, he thought,
Was long and densely shared,
Engulfed
In a matrix,
Undefined,
Its verge the verge of sight.
He plied the pathways of a human form,

Nestled in a soily Earth,
And was as real (by his own account)
As the rising sun,
Enmeshed, and unsurpassed;
He purled,
Trickling time
Into passing words –
What he knew
Swam, buoyant;
He brushed a fern-leaf,
And unfurled,
Soft tips,
Crest-caught,
Sipped at the current's turn.
And he knew,
With each swirl,
That ardour prospered.

Conclusion:

The task that remains, now, is to consider the sum of what has been revealed in the foregoing discussion about the relations between language, experience, and poetic expression. Attention has been given to the technical and aesthetic contracts that allow, in poetry, a creative response amid these relations. The relations themselves have also been briefly examined. Throughout, the concern has been, and is here again, to highlight the uncertainty that is both exposed and contained through creative endeavours. The concern has at once been, and remains, to describe an urge for creative redemption as a response, an elegiac response, to this uncertainty. The discussion closes, here, with a return to mathematics.

Henri Poincaré writes that, "experience does not prove to us that space has three dimensions; it only proves to us that it is convenient to attribute three to it".[216] Acceptance of this uncertainty led, in mathematics, to the development of many new geometries, geometries with fractional, multiple, and infinitely many dimensions.[217] An admission of uncertainty, the example reiterates, can promote intense and rewarding creativity. At a recognised point of indeterminacy, a creator gains the opportunity to give him- or herself over, as Hart has implied, "to the allure of the imaginary".[218] The release into notions of what else might be possible is a prerequisite for the creation of any new work. As has been argued, more is required in this process than uncertainty alone. Indeterminacy achieves nothing without a setting and a discipline through which it can be recognised and responded to. In poetic creativity, language and poetic convention are each sources of both order *and* indeterminacy. In language and in his or her poetic contracts, a poet finds both a centre and an infinite margin, both the support, in other words, and the provocation whereby creativity may seem a possible and a desirable endeavour. Poetic contracts allow poets to give focus and value to that which has not yet been produced, and to sustain a commitment to an emerging poem even when the work involved is difficult or unpleasant. They allow, also, and encourage, both a commitment to and divergence within the field of poetry as an art form. Poetic contracts establish a reference to poetic traditions but are at once negotiable, dynamic documents, unable to stipulate absolutely what it is a poet must do in order to create a new poem. Risks must be taken and the "be me but not me" charge insists that *certain kinds* of risks (though it cannot state which ones) are necessary for the production of a compelling work. A poet, thus equipped, bearing both hope and doubt, may attempt to augment poetic expression, the task being to localise and respond to the indeterminacies that language and poetic conventions yield.

There is no creativity without uncertainty; "the risk of surrendering to the inessential is itself essential", Blanchot writes.[219] Creators create by approaching a dangerous resource. The argument here is that the effort is made with (and not without) the possibility of redemption in mind. Creative redemption is experienced fundamentally as a feeling of power. To write a redeeming poem is to have the power to respond to the absence uncertainty implies. Thus a poet is one who imagines power (borrowing from Blanchot) "even in the region of the ungraspable".[220] It is the power to slide towards impossibility and to become a source of movement returning to deliver what was previously just out of reach. Pure expression is not tapped, language and experience do not meet, but poems are forged. The fullness of presence is not attained, but a poet can occasionally speak with such vigour and persuasion that, while this vigour lingers, the presence of absence pales. In a redeeming poem, fresh means of expression are uncovered and new or renewed concepts and experiences can be unveiled. It is the *capacity* to yield such effects, rather than the effects themselves, that most directly redeems the medium and the mind involved. In the writing of poetry, the known can seem to intersect with the unknown, the possible with the impossible. Through the uncertainty that lends scope, always, for something else, what is ordinary can be rendered less familiar and more immediate. The "imaginary body" that a poem restores "to the abstract bones of language" (in the words of Chris Wallace-Crabbe),[221] becomes a body that draws us back to alertness, a body that seems, momentarily, to be not merely the corpse of an earlier age. The process is one of defamiliarisation, but there is much at stake. In his study of the English elegy, Peter Sacks points to "the elegist's need to draw attention, consolingly, to his own surviving powers".[222] In all poetry, uncertainty offers the same opportunity. We cannot defeat absence, but we can express, consolingly, and in celebration, impressions of a surviving capacity for delivering meaningful effect. The lament finds its balance. In the presence of absence is the possibility of voicing responses peculiar to our time and to ourselves.

Language, experience, and poetic expression are drawn together by a poet's urge to create a compelling poem. There are no natural relations that allow one to serve the other. On the contrary, explicit contrivance in poetry, added to the indefinite relay of signification in language, means that a pure translation of the subjects a poet selects not only fails to become available but is never entirely sought. The experiences that inform a poet's creative efforts are forever distanced by an infinite chain of signifiers *and*, more blatantly, by the desire to produce a work that is recognisably poetic. What is revealed here is that the gap between language and experience, and the playful and deceitful exaggeration of this gap achieved via the forms and ideals of poetry, are what allow, in poetic creativity, the apparent *arrival* of *other* experiences, significant experiences in their own right, both of and apart from that by which they are inspired. Exquisite tangents that at once kill and bring to life. It is from uncertainty, from that which holds being and meaning apart, that the elegiac substitute can be born. The effects a poem produces will not be the same as the experiences the poet recalled or imagined, but this "loss", or transferral, is ideally compensated for by the persuasiveness of what is delivered. Creative redemption, here, subjectively perceived by a poet in relation to his or her knowledge of and preferences within poetry, is never absolute. The poet who writes again, or who writes next, finds no depletion: uncertainties continue to rage, and the poetic machine continues to lend its ear to their incessant whispers. René Char offers, aptly, that, "The poem is the realized love of desire still desiring".[223] Literature, says Blanchot, "is a dishonest and confused experience in which one succeeds only by failing".[224] The perfect and final poem does not arrive. Yet the effort to allow what cannot be said to still be heard continues to be made. The terrible resource Blanchot calls inspiration, the resource of absence, superfluity, and uncertainty, continues to be transformed into yet more and other poems. From between the familiar and the ungraspable are drawn, repeatedly (and without repeat), the relative resolutions that are creativity, each poet proclaiming, in the process, the opportunities and the responsibilities that are contractually his or hers.

Coda: Creativity – the urge and the act

The tenuous arrogance of the desire to inspire others. The feeling of being inspired.
Compulsion. Delight. Loss. Also doubt. All are common companions to creativity. Their stage: a
foreshore. On one side, the dangerous, uncertain sea, full of risk and opportunity. On the other,
the land, its solidity and apparent order. The known and the unknown intersect on a Derridean
threshold. If a creator is not one who can quite bring him or herself to reside here, within reach of
the recurring tides, he or she will at least be a regular visitor, borrowing from the chance for
transformation.

Island

From the verge of dry sand, bracing against the cold,
he steps out, care and impulse in separate hands
as he strides towards the wave-tops.

His glance shoots back
and he's warmed by the rise of familiar stone,
wraps his island round him like a living shawl,

and with this comfort oozing into courage
leans into the ocean's pull.

Though he tries, he cannot gauge the blue horizon,
sky evades water, or water swerves,
and the brawl burrows under – he imagines

a gap of swallowed ground.
He doesn't pause,
falls through the tide's flow, and swims,

stretching into each stroke, rolling
in the salt's swell, frayed by the jagged water.

And rising breathless,
he turns to judge the measure of his daring.
    But nothing's changed.

The sand beneath his feet is the same sand, and the stone
still looms. He digs for purchase, wraps just the shoreline
round his shoulders, and

plunges into swollen waves. Valour, in the fringes
of his faith. He reaches,
    dreading what he might choose.

Vision

tilting the head sideways at the river's waves
to see stones slide into cuneiform.

Nautilus

on the sandbank of his mind, the spirals
of his thought's discarded shells.

Attaining Wisdom

Birds still dreaming
Will wake with memories of my brother's stand,
And since beauty, too, sends shockwaves,
A thrush already singing on the world's other side
Will rise into broader song. Flowers
Gasp into sudden bloom.
I watch him speak, but he does not look at me.
I press his hand. "Is it for all of us", I ask.
He takes "is", its endless strand, and the scent of "all",
But nothing else. "Can I learn to see
What you have seen?" The question lingers.

While he sleeps, and while I cannot sleep,
I watch the jagged rolling of our chests,
And I do not love him.
I see the curve of his covered eyes
That are also my eyes, and I see his lips
Thin without the whispers of his words.
And but for pulse, he is empty.
The thrush recants.
By morning, birds have all forgotten,
And I climb into daylight as an only child,
Lured
        by the faint touch of flowers.

Revolution:

the door off its hinges:
>an angle of sun
the house has
never seen,
>crawls across the carpet.

Midnight

A woman faces stars,

night's silence
in her reedy spine. She

reaches into black.

The candle
of her flesh

gently burns.

Impact:

we embrace, convinced we'll remember,
the views the mountain path
held till our arrival, returning to slide

into borrowed scenes
the imprint of ourselves.

From his room,

all fusion appeared defensible:
gums breathed into paling blue, and their leaves
were the sound of water; the river

moved inside his palms, and the silence
of his four walls became the day.
Seeping through porous glass,

he looks for shadows from the noise of himself
and for the hues of his slant of mind,
returning

to translate what he finds:
the music
all in curves.

Symphonic Dance

The mind's players
loiter in a subway,
instruments in their mouths – there's
no real orchestra:
the oboist
breaks off in mid
note, sidesteps two metres and
starts all over;
there are violinists
moving on and off the carriages.
And what
startles, broken but
still heard,
is the music.

A snare drummer,
catching the promise,
sets up on the second platform,
and waits
but isn't cued:
The conductor
stands on a rostrum
on the tracks
of an
empty line;
the top flick of the
baton
gives time its
limping order, but

she's hard to see.
The drummer leaves,
returns on a

different train for a
better view,
and when he plays,
shadows
in the notes
            trace
    swells
        of a fuller sound:

the conductor
            insists she nears
    the moment of
blooming, she
        dreams of
        the ecstatic
                    rise, the
            almost-
            pain
She conducts,
    quivering
        with a rhythm
    no-one plays: she
        feels the rumblings,
    relayed through the
            line,
of what rides, and rides alone,
    as death. She finds
        the auguries
        of hope
        in air
    over tearing winds,

        and she names her chance:
to out-sound the roaring
    of impending end.

Redemption

the haiku
alights on a tenderness
you thought had died.

the artist pretends to feel

pushing against the bark, the tip of the penknife
already sticky, resisted by the viscous sap,
she's not carving her name;

she's tapping what the thick, dead skin
hides in its covered veins,
and it's not the amber, clotting as she digs,

but the empty channel, from root to branch,
and the drop, then, of her own blood
to fill the aridity.

Behind a poet in the dole queue:

a hint of faith, losing its nerve, takes 1.72 years
to state its desired occupation.

Cave Art

To press into stone the promise of unyielding rage,
From the crucible of the flesh, the hand
In the flickering of our thin flame. From the mouth,
The still-warm paint.

tilt

the yellow dune
changing its skin, changing its skin,
what beautiful sand

In the middle of things

wings
without feathers,
the broken shell.

infringement

it is love that robs from me, spilling from her lips to mine
what I cannot reach alone; quarried from within me,

a distilled heat that burns around nothing:
she's pouring light

through the tissue of my lungs, and the suffocation
draws her figure on my skin, like dew

curving out of empty skies, the imprint of her hand
passing through me.

    Stay,

       …let the rhythm of your sigh
    rise against my will   and lead me

to the tremble of your plunder.

ENDNOTES:

[1] Maurice Blanchot (1949), tr. Lydia Davis (n.d.), "Literature and the Right to Death", in *The Work of Fire*, Maurice Blanchot (1949), tr. Charlotte Mandell (1995), Stanford University Press, Stanford, p. 322.

[2] Jacques Derrida, tr. Barbara Harlow (1978), *Spurs: Nietzsche's Styles*, University of Chicago Press, Chicago, p. 119.

[3] Jacques Derrida, "Living On: *Border Lines*", in *Deconstruction and Criticism*, Harold Bloom, Paul de Man, Jacques Derrida, Geoffrey Hartman, and J. Hillis Miller (1979), Seabury, New York, p. 78.

[4] Jacques Derrida, in the interview "Jacques Derrida", *Criticism in Society: Interviews*, Imre Salusinsky, ed./interviewer (1987), Methuen, New York, p. 20.

[5] Jeremy Hawthorn (2000), *A Glossary of Contemporary Literary Theory*, 4th edn., Arnold, London, p. 82.

[6] Jacques Derrida (1972), tr. Alan Bass (1982), *Margins of Philosophy*, Harvester Press, Brighton, p. 318.

[7] Jacques Derrida (1967), tr. Gayatri Chakravorty Spivak (1997), *Of Grammatology*, Corrected Edition, Johns Hopkins University Press, Baltimore, p. 159.

[8] Madan Sarup (1988), *An Introductory Guide to Post-Structuralism and Postmodernism*, Harvester Wheatsheaf, London, p. 36.

[9] Ann Smock, "Introduction", in *The Space of Literature*, Maurice Blanchot, tr. Ann Smock (1982), University of Nebraska Press, Lincoln, p. 14.

[10] See Kevin Hart (2004), *The Dark Gaze: Maurice Blanchot and the Sacred*, University of Chicago Press, Chicago, in press.

[11] Derrida, tr. Spivak (1967/97), p. 154.

[12] *Ibid.*, p. 283.

[13] Maurice Blanchot (1955), tr. Ann Smock (1982), *The Space of Literature*, University of Nebraska Press, Lincoln, p. 143.

[14] Maurice Blanchot (1969), tr. Susan Hanson (1993), *The Infinite Conversation*, University of Minnesota Press, Minneapolis, p. 207.

[15] Blanchot, tr. Davis, "Literature and the Right to Death", in Blanchot, tr. Mandell (1949/95), p. 324.

[16] Stuart Sim (1992), *Beyond Aesthetics: Confrontations with Poststructuralism and Postmodernism*, University of Toronto Press, Toronto, p. 41.

[17] *Ibid.*, p. 136.

[18] Richard Kearney (1984), "Dialogue with Jacques Derrida: Deconstruction and the other", *Dialogues with Contemporary Continental Thinkers: The Phenomenological Heritage*, Manchester University Press, Manchester, p. 114.

[19] Vincent B. Leitch (1983), *Deconstructive Criticism: An Advanced Introduction*, Columbia University Press, New York, p. 41.

[20] Kevin Hart, "The Experience of Poetry", in *Boxkite: A Journal of Poetry and Poetics*, 2 (1998), p. 299.

[21] Jacques Derrida (1974), tr. John P. Leavey, Jr. and Richard Rand (1986), *Glas*, University of Nebraska Press, Lincoln, p. 262, col. 1.

[22] Derrida, tr. Bass (1972/82), p. 11.

[23] This is not a concern carried by all forms of deconstruction. For many American proponents, Paul de Man and Geoffrey Hartman, for example, the deconstructive act leads only to more deconstruction. A consuming and exclusive appreciation of, or meditation on, the deconstructive act privileges, as Harold Bloom suggests, the trope at the expense of the troper (Bloom (1977), p. 392-3). The *implications* of play are swallowed by the processes of constructing evidence for its existence; undecidability effectively becomes the new and only centre. The process can lead nowhere but to a (necessarily false) representation of marginality. Barbara Johnson concludes that, "whatever else we may be doing, we are at any rate being 'done in' by our own words" (Johnson (1980), p. 66). This would not seem to be Derrida's line of thought.

[24] Jacques Derrida (1967) tr. Alan Bass (1978), "Structure, Sign and Play in the Discourse of the Human Sciences", *Writing and Difference*, University of Chicago Press, Chicago, p. 292.

[25] Jacques Derrida, ed. Derek Attridge (1992), *Acts of Literature*, Routledge, New York, p. 47.

[26] Derrida, tr. Bass (1967/78), "Ellipsis", p. 297.

[27] Derrida, tr. Bass (1967/78), "Structure, Sign and Play in the Discourse of the Human Sciences", p. 279.

[28] Vincent Leitch (1983), *Deconstructive Criticism: An Advanced Introduction*, Columbia University Press, New York, p. 246.

[29] Sim (1992), p. 49.

[30] Kevin Hart, "The Experience of Poetry", in *Boxkite: A Journal of Poetry and Poetics*, 2 (1998), p. 301.

[31] Friedrich Nietzsche, tr. Francis Golffing (1956), *The Birth of Tragedy and The Genealogy of Morals*, Doubleday, New York, p. 65.

[32] Friedrich Nietzsche, tr. R.J. Hollingdale (1979), intro. Michael Tanner (1992), *Ecce Homo*, Penguin, London, pp. 51-2.

[33] Michael Serres (1986), tr. Genevieve James and Raymond Federman (1989), *Detachment*, Ohio University Press, Athens, pp. 10-11.

[34] Michel Serres (1982), quoted by Maria L. Assad, "Michel Serres: In Search of a Tropography", in *Chaos and Order; Complex Dynamics in Literature and Science*, N. Katherine Hayles, ed. (1991), University of Chicago Press, Chicago, p. 286 (Assad cites the French edn; a less revealing translation of the passage is given in Michel Serres (1982), tr. Genevieve James and James Nielson (1995), *Genesis*, University of Michigan Press, Ann Arbor).

[35] Maria Assad, "Michel Serres: In Search of a Tropography", in *Chaos and Order: Complex Dynamics in Literature and Science*, N. Katherine Hayles, ed. (1991), University of Chicago Press, Chicago, p. 283.

[36] Blanchot, tr. Smock (1955/82), p. 142.

[37] Alasdair MacIntyre (1985), *After Virtue: A Study in Moral Theory*, 2nd edn., Duckworth, London, p. 216.

[38] Jean-François Lyotard, tr. David Macey, "Lessons in paganism" in *The Lyotard Reader*, Andrew Benjamin, ed. (1989), Basil Blackwell, Cambridge, p. 137.

[39] Blanchot, tr. Smock (1955/82), p. 179.

[40] Lyn Hejinian (1992), *The Cell*, Sun & Moon, Los Angeles, p. 120.

[41] Derrida, tr. Bass (1967/78), "Structure, Sign and Play in the Discourse of the Human Science", p. 280.

[42] Terry Eagleton (1990), *The Ideology of the Aesthetic*, Basil Blackwell, Oxford, p. 351.

[43] Thom Gunn (1982), "Writing a Poem" (1973) in *The Occasions of Poetry: Essays in Criticism and Autobiography*, Clive Wilmer, ed., North Point Press, San Francisco, p. 162.

[44] Christopher Norris (1991), *Deconstruction: Theory and Practice*, Routledge, London, p. 115.

[45] Blanchot, tr. Davis, "Literature and the Right to Death", in Blanchot, tr. Mandell (1949/95), p. 329.

[46] *Ibid.*, p. 327.

[47] Eagleton (1990), p. 341.

[48] Alex Skovron (1992), "Quadrilateral", in *Sleeve Notes*, Hale & Iremonger, Sydney, p. 35.

[49] Blanchot, tr. Smock (1955/82), p. 184.

[50] W.S. Graham, "Notes on a Poetry of Release" in *Strong Words: Modern Poets on Modern Poetry*, W.N. Herbert and Matthew Hollis, eds. (2000), Bloodaxe, Tarset, Northumberland, p. 118.

[51] Jacques Derrida, "Living On: *Border Lines*", in *Deconstruction and Criticism*, Harold Bloom, Paul de Man, Jacques Derrida, Geoffrey Hartman, and J. Hillis Miller (1979), Seabury, New York, p. 116.

[52] *Ibid.*, p. 117.

[53] Derrida, tr. Leavey and Rand (1974/86), p. 262, col. 1.

[54] Kevin Hart, "The Experience of Poetry", in *Boxkite: A Journal of Poetry and Poetics*, 2 (1998), p. 294.

[55] Adrienne Rich, "Poetry and Experience: Statement at a Poetry Reading" in Herbert and Hollis (2000), p. 142.

[56] W.H. Auden, "The Virgin and the Dynamo" in Herbert and Hollis (2000), p. 70.

[57] T.S. Eliot, "Tradition and the Individual Talent" (1919) in *Selected Prose of T.S. Eliot*, Frank Kermode, ed. (1975), Faber and Faber, London, p. 40.

[58] James Engell (1981), *The Creative Imagination: Enlightenment to Romanticism*, Harvard University Press, Cambridge, MA, p. 288.

[59] Ted Hughes, "Words and Experience" in Herbert and Hollis (2000), pp. 154, 153.

[60] Blanchot, tr. Smock (1955/82), p. 87.

[61] John Forbes, *Collected Poems: 1970-1998*, Brandl & Schlesinger, New South Wales, p. 27.

[62] Kevin Hart, "The Experience of Poetry", in *Boxkite: A Journal of Poetry and Poetics*, 2 (1998), p. 300.

[63] Blanchot, tr. Smock (1955/82), p. 141.
[64] *Ibid.*, p. 178.
[65] Derrida, tr. Bass (1967/78), "Structure, Sign and Play in the Discourse of the Human Sciences", p. 292.
[66] Kevin Hart (2004), *The Dark Gaze: Maurice Blanchot and the Sacred*, University of Chicago Press, Chicago, in press.
[67] *Ibid.*
[68] Wallace Stevens (1951), *The Necessary Angel: Essays on reality and the imagination*, Vintage, New York, p. 175.
[69] Derrida, tr. Bass (1967/78), "Structure, Sign and Play in the Discourse of the Human Sciences", p. 293.
[70] Blanchot, tr. Smock (1955/82), pp. 242-3.
[71] William Stafford (1976) in "Interview with William Stafford", *The World's Hieroglyphic Beauty: Five American Poets*, Peter Stitt (1985), University of Georgia Press, Athens, p. 101.
[72] Brendan Kennelly, "Voices" in Herbert and Hollis (2000), p. 214.
[73] Robert Penn Warren (1977), in "Interview with Robert Penn Warren", Stitt (1985), p. 249.
[74] Harold Bloom (1982), *Agon: Towards a Theory of Revisionism*, Oxford University Press, New York, p. 250.
[75] Kevin Hart, "The Experience of Poetry", in *Boxkite: A Journal of Poetry and Poetics*, 2 (1998), p. 291.
[76] *Ibid.*, p. 292.
[77] Ann Smock, in her introduction to Blanchot, tr. Smock (1955/82), p. 9.
[78] Jahan Ramazani (1994), *Poetry of Mourning: The Modern Elegy from Hardy to Heaney*, University of Chicago Press, Chicago, p. 119.
[79] Wallace Stevens, "Notes Towards a Supreme Fiction" in *The Palm at the End of the Mind: Selected Poems and a Play*, Holly Stevens, ed. (1971), Vintage, New York, p. 225.
[80] *Ibid.*, p. 228.
[81] *Ibid.*, p. 158 ("The Poems of Our Climate").
[82] Blanchot, tr. Smock (1955/82), p. 106.
[83] *Ibid.*, p. 87.
[84] Fagan (2002), pp. 15, 39.
[85] Donald Justice (1995), "The Artist Orpheus", *New & Selected Poems*, Knopf, New York, p. 4.
[86] Gaston Bachelard (1958), tr. Maria Jolas (1964), *The Poetics of Space*, Beacon, Boston, p. 80.
[87] Christopher Herold, in Bill Sewell and Jeanette Stace, eds. (1991), *Balancing on Blue*, The New Zealand Poetry Society, Wellington, p. 43.
[88] Raymond Roseliep (1980), *Listen to Light*, Alembic, Ithaca, New York, p. 47.
[89] John Forbes, "Egyptian Reggae", *Collected Poems: 1970-1998*, Brandl & Schlesinger, New South Wales, p. 127.
[90] Victor Shklovsky, "Art as Technique", in *Russian Formalist Criticism: Four Essays*, Lee T. Lemon and Marion J. Reis, eds/trs (1965), University of Nebraska Press, Lincoln, p. 22.
[91] *Ibid.*, p. 12.
[92] *Ibid.*
[93] This comment bears the influence of the work of Søren Kierkegaard. Irony, in Kierkegaard's broad use of the term, is "the bath of regeneration and rejuvenation" and "redeems the soul from having its life in finitude though living boldly and energetically *in* finitude" (Søren Kierkegaard, tr. Lee M. Capel (1965), *The Concept of Irony*, Indiana University Press, Bloomington, p. 339). A poet's lies are ironies by Kierkegaard's definition.
[94] Blanchot, tr. Davis, "Literature and the Right to Death", in Blanchot, tr. Mandell (1949/95), p. 330.
[95] *Ibid.*, p. 310.
[96] Arthur Koestler (1964), *The Act of Creation*, The Danube Edition (1969), Hutchinson, London, p. 380.
[97] Samual Taylor Coleridge (1808), "Shakespeare's Judgment Equal to His Genius", in *Shakespearean Criticism*, vol. 1, Thomas Middleton Raysor, ed. (1960), Dent, London, p. 197.
[98] Frank Kermode (1968), *Continuities*, Random House, New York, p. 22.
[99] David Lehman (1987), *Ecstatic Occasions, Expedient Forms: 65 Leading Contemporary Poets Select and Comment on Their Poems*, Macmillan, New York, p. 215.
[100] Wallace Stevens, "Adagia" (1934-1940?), in *Opus Posthumous by Wallace Stevens: Poems, Plays, Prose*, revised edn., Milton J. Bates, ed. (1989), Vintage, New York, p. 200.

[101] A.R. Ammons (1974), *Sphere: The Form of a Motion*, Norton, New York, p. 25.

[102] Blanchot, tr. Smock (1955/82), p. 182.

[103] Igor Stravinsky, tr. Arthur Knodel and Ingolf Dahl (1947), *Poetics of Music in the form of Six Lessons*, Random House, New York, p. 68.

[104] John Ashbery, "Variation on a Noel", in Lehman (1987), p. 5.

[105] Richard Kenney, "from 'The Encantadas'", in Lehman (1987), p. 115.

[106] Koestler (1964), p. 343.

[107] Paul Valéry, tr. Jackson Mathews (1940), "The Course in Poetics: First Lesson", in *The Creative Process: A Symposium*", Brewster Ghiselin, ed. (1952), Mentor, New York, p. 104.

[108] Louis Zukofsky (1981), "A Statement for Poetry", in *Prepositions: The Collected Critical Essays of Louis Zukofsky*, expanded edn., University of California Press, Berkeley, p. 23.

[109] Alex Preminger and T.V.F. Brogan, eds. (1993), "Poetics", in *The New Princeton Encyclopedia of Poetry and Poetics*, Princeton University Press, Princeton, p. 933, col. 1.

[110] Charles Olson, "Projective Verse", in Herbert and Hollis (2000), p. 93.

[111] Molly Peacock, "She Lays", in (1987), p. 158.

[112] John Tranter (1977), "20", *Crying in Early Infancy: 100 Sonnets*, Makar, Brisbane, p.17.

[113] Alan Williamson (1994), *Eloquence and Mere Life: Essays on the Art of Poetry*, University of Michigan Press, Ann Arbor, p. 147.

[114] Robert Creeley, "From an Interview with Linda Wagner", in Lammon (1996), p. 62.

[115] A.R. Ammons, "Guide", in Lehman (1987), p. 216.

[116] Robert Brown, "Creativity, What Are We To Measure?", in *The Handbook of Creativity*, John A. Glover, Royce R. Ronning and Cecil R. Reynolds, eds. (1989), Plenum, New York, p. 3.

[117] Seamus Heaney, "Craft and Technique" in Herbert and Hollis (2000), p. 159.

[118] Anthony Hecht, "Meditation", in Lehman (1987), p. 81.

[119] Richard Kenney, "from 'The Encantadas'", in Lehman (1987), p. 115.

[120] Richard Wilbur (1977), in "Interview with Richard Wilbur", Stitt (1985), p. 50.

[121] David Lehman, "Notes on Poetic Form", in Lammon (1996), p. 47.

[122] Molly Peacock, "She Lays", in Lehman (1987), p. 157.

[123] William Stafford (1976), in "Interview with William Stafford", Stitt (1985), p. 102.

[124] *Ibid.*, p. 103.

[125] e.e. cummings (1962), *73 poems*, Faber & Faber, London, poem "66".

[126] Amiri Baraka, "How You Sound??", in Herbert and Hollis (2000), pp. 135-6.

[127] Eliot Weinberger, "A Note on *Montemora*, America and the World", *Sulfur* 20 (Fall 1987), p. 197.

[128] Fred D'Aguiar, "Further Adventures in the Skin Trade", in Herbert and Hollis (2000), p. 272.

[129] James Wright (1972), in "Interview with James Wright", Stitt (1985), p. 207.

[130] Laurie Duggan in "An Interview with Laurie Duggan", David McCooey, in *The Literary Review*, 45.1 (2001), p. 134.

[131] Kevin Brophy (1998), *Creativity: Psychoanalysis, Surrealism and Creative Writing*, Melbourne University Press, Melbourne, p. 133.

[132] Robert Epstein (1996), *Cognition, Creativity, and Behavior: Selected Essays*, Praeger, Westport, p. 59.

[133] John Hayes, "Cognitive Processes in Creativity", in Glover, Ronning, and Reynolds (1989), p. 140.

[134] Morton Feldman in *Give My Regards to Eighth Street: Collected Writings of Morton Feldman*, B.H. Friedman, ed. (2000), Exact Change, Cambridge, p. 134.

[135] Colin Martindale, "Personality, Situation, and Creativity", in Glover, Ronning, and Reynolds (1989), p. 219.

[136] Epstein (1996), p. 54.

[137] Feldman ed. Friedman (2000), p. 23.

[138] *Ibid.*, p. 209.

[139] Susan Sontag (1969), *Styles of Radical Will*, Vintage, London, p. 5.

[140] Feldman ed. Friedman (2000), p. 41.

[141] *Ibid.*, p. 111.

[142] Jacques Derrida, tr. Mary Quaintance, "Force of Law: 'The Mystical Foundation of Authority'", in *Deconstruction and the Possibility of Justice*, Drucilla Cornell, Michel Rosenfeld, and David Gray Carlson, eds. (1992), Routledge, New York, p. 20.

[143] John Kinsella, "Almost a Dialogue with Lyn Hejinian: Quotations and Phantom Limbs..." in Herbert and Hollis (2000), p. 205.

[144] Lloyd Motz and Jefferson Hane Weaver (1993), *The Story of Mathematics*, Plenum, New York, p. 330.

[145] Michael Guillen (1995), *Five Equations that Changed the World*, Little, Brown & Company, London, p. 6.

[146] Richard Wilbur (1977), in "Interview with Richard Wilbur", Stitt (1985), p. 50.

[147] *Ibid.*

[148] James Voss and Mary Means, "Towards a Model of Creativity Based upon Problem Solving in the Social Sciences", in Glover, Ronning, and Reynolds (1989), p. 404.

[149] Miller Mair (1989), *Between Psychology and Psychotherapy: A Poetics of Experience*, Routledge, London, p. 77.

[150] Craig Raine quoted by Lehman (1987), p. 49 (no reference given by Lehman).

[151] Blanchot, tr. Smock (1955/82), p. 143.

[152] Blanchot, tr. Mandell (1949/95), "Gazes from Beyond the Grave", p. 245.

[153] Blanchot, tr. Smock (1955/82), p. 183.

[154] Mair (1989), p. 235.

[155] Koestler (1964), p. 165 (Poincaré is quoted on the same page).

[156] James Voss and Mary Means, "Toward a Model of Creativity Based upon Problem Solving in the Social Sciences" in Glover, Ronning, and Reynolds (1989), p. 409.

[157] Eliot ed. Kermode (1975), p. 39.

[158] Kevin Hart, "The Experience of Poetry", in *Boxkite: A Journal of Poetry and Poetics*, 2 (1998), p. 292.

[159] Feldman ed. Friedman (2000), p. 47.

[160] Bloom (1982), p. 114.

[161] Alicia Suskin Ostriker (2000), *Dancing at the Devil's Party: Essays on Poetry, Politics, and the Erotic*, University of Michigan Press, Ann Arbor, p. 31.

[162] Bloom (1982), p. viii.

[163] Terry Eagleton (1996), *Literary Theory: An Introduction*, 2nd edn., Blackwell, Oxford, p. 159.

[164] Harold Bloom (1973), *The Anxiety of Influence: A Theory of Poetry*, Oxford University Press, New York, p. 70.

[165] Blanchot, tr. Davis, "Literature and the Right to Death", in Blanchot, tr. Mandell (1949/95), p. 314.

[166] Bloom (1973), p. 154.

[167] Bloom (1982), p. 171.

[168] Bloom (1973), p. 58.

[169] Kevin Hart, "The Experience of Poetry", in *Boxkite: A Journal of Poetry and Poetics*, 2 (1998), p. 294.

[170] Bloom (1973), p. 50.

[171] Bloom (1982), p. 98.

[172] *Ibid.*, p. 120.

[173] Percy Bysshe Shelley, "Defence of Poetry" in *The Four Ages of Poetry: Peacock's Four Ages of Poetry, Shelley's Defence of Poetry, Browning's Essay on Shelley*, H.F.B. Brett-Smith, ed. (1972), Basil Blackwell, Oxford, p. 33.

[174] Victor Shklovsky, "Art as Technique" in Lemon and Reis (1965), p. 12.

[175] Yves Bonnefoy, tr. John Naughton (1991), "Interview with Yves Bonnefoy" (conducted by Naughton), *In the Shadow's Light: with an interview with Yves Bonnefoy*, University of Chicago Press, Chicago, p. 162.

[176] Charles Wright, "Improvisations on Form and Measure", in Lammon (1996), p. 28.

[177] Wallace Stevens, "Man Carrying Thing", in Stevens (1971), p. 281.

[178] Wallace Stevens, "Of Mere Being", "Reality Is an Activity of the Most August Imagination", "Extracts from Addresses to the Academy of Fine Ideas", in Stevens (1971), pp. 398, 396, 178, respectively.

[179] Alan Wearne (October 14 1999), "Conversations with a Dead Poet", in *Sunday Afternoon*, Australian Broadcasting Corporation (television documentary).

[180] Theodore Roethke, "In a Dark Time", in *The American Tradition in Literature*, 8th edn., George Perkins and Barbara Perkins, eds. (1994), McGraw-Hill, New York, p. 1705.

[181] e.e. cummings, "If There Are Any Heavens", in *The American Tradition in Literature*, 8th edn., George Perkins and Barbara Perkins, eds. (1994), McGraw-Hill, New York, p. 1476.

[182] Fred D'Aguiar, "Further Adventures in the Skin Trade", in Herbert and Hollis (2000), p. 270.

[183] Williamson (1994), p. 155.

[184] Paul Magnuson, "The Shaping of 'Fears in Solitude'", in *Coleridge's Theory of Imagination Today*, Christine Gallant, ed. (1989), AMS, New York, p. 197-8.

[185] Ramazani (1994), p. ix.

[186] Marjorie Perloff (1991), *Radical Artifice: Writing Poetry in the Age of Media*, University of Chicago Press, Chicago, pp. 47, 57.

[187] Félix Guattari (1992), tr. Paul Bains and Julian Pefanis (1995), *Chaosmosis: An Ethico-Aesthetic Paradigm*, Power Publications, Sydney, p. 36.

[188] Rosemary Huisman (1998), *The Written Poem: Semiotic Conventions from Old to Modern English*, Cassell, London, p. 20.

[189] Simon Karlinsky (1985), *Marina Tsvetaeva: The Woman, her World and her Poetry*, Cambridge University Press, Cambridge, p. 113.

[190] Timothy Bahti and Marilyn Sibley Fries, eds. (1995), *Jewish Writers, German Literature: The Uneasy Examples of Nelly Sachs and Walter Benjamin*, University of Michigan Press, Ann Arbor, pp. 2-4.

[191] Laurie Duggan in "An Interview with Laurie Duggan", David McCooey, in *The Literary Review*, 45.1 (2001), p. 137.

[192] Philip Larkin (1983), "Statement" (1955), in *Required Writing: Miscellaneous Pieces 1955-1982*, Faber & Faber, London, p. 79.

[193] Reuben Hersh (1997), *What Is Mathematics, Really?*, Oxford University Press, New York, p. 136.

[194] When Karl Friedrich Gauss, in the early 1800s, began exploring geometrical ideas that were non-Euclidean, he did not attempt to publish his results. A little later, Nikolai Lobachevsky and Janos Bolyai published independent non-Euclidean findings, but acceptance was not forthcoming. The ideas elicited, writes Michael Monastyrsky, "wild fury from a majority of philosophers" (Monastyrsky (1987), p. 64). Kant had described Euclidean geometry as an unavoidable, innate intuition of the human mind; his followers held that there could be no other (Hersh (1997), p. 263; also Henderson (1983), p. 11; and Burton (1997), p. 542.). Interest and regard for *non*-Euclidean geometries were finally secured, one hundred years after Gauss, through the work of Einstein, whose application of the non-Euclidean mathematics of Georg Riemann illustrated that the new geometries could yield relevant measurements of the physical universe.

[195] Linda Dalrymple Henderson (1983), *The Fourth Dimension & Non-Euclidean Geometry in Modern Art*, Princeton University Press, Princeton, p. 17.

[196] Hersh (1997), p. 70.

[197] Philip Davis, Reuben Hersh, and Elena Anne Marchisotto (1995), *The Mathematical Experience, Study Edition*, Birkhäuser, Boston, p. 363.

[198] Feldman ed. Friedman (2000), p. 22.

[199] Mair (1989), p. 285.

[200] Eagleton (1990), p. 263.

[201] Donald Justice (1984), *Platonic Scripts*, University of Michigan Press, Ann Arbor, p. 152.

[202] *Ibid.*, p. 158.

[203] Suzanne Benack, Michael Basseches, and Thomas Swan, "Dialectical Thinking and Adult Creativity", in Glover, Ronning, and Reynolds (1989), p. 205.

[204] Colin Martindale, "Personality, Situation, and Creativity" in Glover, Ronning, and Reynolds (1989), p. 223.

[205] John Keats in *Letters of John Keats*, Stanley Gardner, ed. (1965), University of London Press, London, p. 68.

[206] Blanchot, tr. Smock (1955/82), p. 184.

[207] *Ibid.*

[208] Eagleton (1990), p. 255.

[209] James Voss and Mary Means, "Toward a Model of Creativity Based upon Problem Solving in the Social Sciences", in Glover, Ronning, and Reynolds (1989), p. 403.

[210] Blanchot, tr. Smock (1955/82), p. 88.

[211] Blanchot, tr. Mandell (1949/95), "René Char", p. 110.

[212] Robert Prentky, "Creativity and Psychopathology", in Glover, Ronning, and Reynolds (1989), p. 247.

[213] Joyce Vantassel-Baska, "The Talent Development Process in Women Writers: A Study of Charlotte Bronte and Virginia Woolf" in *Remarkable Women: Perspectives on Female Talent Development*, Karen Arnold, Kathleen D. Noble, and Rena F. Subotnik, eds. (1996), Hampton Press, Cresskill, p. 296.

[214] Virginia Woolf, ed. Leonard Woolf (1954), *A Writer's Diary: being extracts from the diary of Virginia Woolf*, Harcourt Brace Jovanovich, New York, p. 351.

[215] Mair (1989), p. 245.

[216] Henri Poincaré (1905), tr. George Bruce Halsted (1913, this edn. 1958), "Space and its Three Dimensions", *The Value of Science*, Dover, New York, p. 69.

[217] Carl B. Boyer (1991), *A History of Mathematics*, 2nd edn., Wiley, New York, pp. 520-1, 545-7; also John Allen Paulos (1991), *Beyond Numeracy: An Uncommon Dictionary of Mathematics*, Viking, London, p. 86.

[218] Kevin Hart, "The Experience of Poetry", in *Boxkite: A Journal of Poetry and Poetics*, 2 (1998), p. 294.

[219] Blanchot, tr. Smock (1955/82), p. 169.

[220] *Ibid.*, p. 106.

[221] Chris Wallace-Crabbe (1990), *Poetry and Belief*, University of Tasmania (Occasional Paper, 49), Hobart, p. 13.

[222] Peter Sacks (1985), *The English Elegy: Studies in the Genre from Spenser to Yeats*, Johns Hopkins University Press, Baltimore, p. 2.

[223] René Char quoted by Blanchot, tr. Smock (1955/82), p. 187 (no reference given by Blanchot).

[224] Blanchot, tr. Mandell (1949/95), "Gide and the Literature of Experience", p. 224.

BIBLIOGRAPHY:

Abrams, M.H. (1999), *A Glossary of Literary Terms*, 7ᵗʰ edn., Harcourt Brace College, New York.

Allison, Alexander W., et al., eds. (1970), *The Norton Anthology of Poetry*, 3ʳᵈ edn., Norton, New York.

Ammons, A.R. (1971), *Briefings: Poems Small and Easy*, Norton, New York.

_____ (1974), *Sphere: The Form of a Motion*, Norton, New York.

Annual Review of Fluid Mechanics, 24 (1992), "Wavelet transforms and their applications to turbulence", pp. 395-457.

Arnold, Karen, Noble, Kathleen D., and Subotnik, Rena F., eds. (1996), *Remarkable Women: Perspectives on Female Talent Development*, Hampton Press, Cresskill.

Bachelard, Gaston (1958), tr. Jolas, Maria (1964), *The Poetics of Space*, Beacon, Boston.

Bahti, Timothy and Sibley Fries, Marilyn, eds. (1995), *Jewish Writers, German Literature: The Uneasy Examples of Nelly Sachs and Walter Benjamin*, University of Michigan Press, Ann Arbor.

Baker, Peter (1995), *Deconstruction and the Ethical Turn*, University Press of Florida, Gainesville.

Belgrad, David (1998), *The Culture of Spontaneity, Improvisation and the Arts in Postwar America*, University of Chicago Press, Chicago.

Benjamin, Andrew, ed. (1989), *The Lyotard Reader*, Basil Blackwell, Cambridge.

Blanchot, Maurice (1949), tr. Mandell, Charlotte (1995), *The Work of Fire*, Stanford University Press, Stanford.

_____ (1955), tr. Smock, Ann (1982), *The Space of Literature*, University of Nebraska Press, Lincoln.

_____ (1969), tr. Hanson, Susan (1993), *The Infinite Conversation*, University of Minnesota Press, Minneapolis.

Bloom, Harold (1973), *The Anxiety of Influence: A Theory of Poetry*, Oxford University Press, New York.

_____ (1977), *Wallace Stevens: The Poems of Our Climate*, Cornell University Press, London.

_____ (1982), *Agon: Towards a Theory of Revisionism*, Oxford University Press, New York.

_____ (1982b), *The Breaking of the Vessels*, University of Chicago Press, Chicago.

Bloom, Harold, de Man, Paul, Derrida, Jacques, Hartman, Geoffrey, and Hillis Miller, J. (1979), *Deconstruction and Criticism*, Seabury, New York.

Blyth, R.H. (1949), *Haiku*, vol.1, Hokuseido Press, Tokyo.

Boxkite: A Journal of Poetry and Poetics, 2 (1998), "The Experience of Poetry", pp. 285-304.

Boyer, Carl B. (1991), *A History of Mathematics*, 2nd edn., Wiley, New York.

Brett-Smith. H.F.B., ed. (1972), *The Four Ages of Poetry: Peacock's Four Ages of Poetry, Shelley's Defence of Poetry, Browning's Essay on Shelley*, Basil Blackwell, Oxford.

Brophy, Kevin (1998), *Creativity: Psychoanalysis, Surrealism and Creative Writing*, Melbourne University Press, Melbourne.

Carroll, John (1998), *Ego and Soul: The Modern West in Search of Meaning*, HarperCollins, Sydney.

Coleridge, Samuel Taylor (1906 edn.), *Biographia Literaria*, Dent, London and Dutton, New York.

_____, Raysor, Thomas Middleton, ed. (1960), *Shakespearean Criticism*, vol. 1, Dent, London.

Cornell, Drucilla, Rosenfeld, Michel and Carlson, David Gray, eds. (1992), *Deconstruction and the Possibility of Justice*, Routledge, New York.

cummings, e.e. (1962), *73 poems*, Faber & Faber, London.

Davis, Philip, Hersh, Reuben and Marchisotto, Elena (1995), *The Mathematical Experience*, Study Edition, Birkhäuser, Boston.

Derrida, Jacques (1967), tr. Bass, Alan (1978), *Writing and Difference*, University of Chicago Press, Chicago.

_____ (1967), tr. Spivak, Gayatri Chakravorty (1997), *Of Grammatology*, Corrected Edition, Johns Hopkins University Press, Baltimore.

_____ (1972), tr. Bass, Alan (1982), *Margins of Philosophy*, Harvester Press, Brighton.

_____ (1974), tr. Leavey, John P., Jr. and Rand, Richard (1986), *Glas*, University of Nebraska Press, Lincoln.

_____ tr. Harlow, Barbara (1978), *Spurs: Nietzsche's Styles*, University of Chicago Press, Chicago.

_____ ed. Attridge, Derek (1992), *Acts of Literature*, Routledge, New York.

Dews, Peter (1987), *Logics of Disintegration: Post-Structuralist Thought and the Claims of Critical Theory*, Verso, London.

Eagleton, Terry (1990), *The Ideology of the Aesthetic*, Basil Blackwell, Oxford.

_____ (1996), *Literary Theory: An Introduction*, 2nd edn., Blackwell, Oxford.

Engell, James (1981), *The Creative Imagination: Enlightenment to Romanticism*, Harvard University Press, Cambridge, MA.

Epstein, Robert (1996), *Cognition, Creativity, and Behavior: Selected Essays*, Praeger, Westport.

Forbes, John, *Collected Poems: 1970-1998*, Brandl & Schlesinger, Rose Bay, New South Wales.

Friedman, B.H., ed. (2000), *Give My Regards to Eighth Street: Collected Writings of Morton Feldman*, Exact Change, Cambridge.

Gallant, Christine, ed. (1989) *Coleridge's Theory of Imagination Today*, AMS, New York.

Gardner, Howard (1993) *Creating Minds: An Anatomy of Creativity*, Basic, New York.

Gardner, Stanley, ed. (1965), *Letters of John Keats*, University of London Press, London.

Ghiselin, Brewster, ed. (1952), *The Creative Process: A Symposium"*, Mentor, New York.

Glover, John A., Ronning, Royce R. and Reynolds, Cecil R., eds. (1989), *The Handbook of Creativity*, Plenum, New York.

Guattari, Félix (1992), tr. Bains, Paul and Pefanis, Julian (1995), *Chaosmosis: An Ethico-Aesthetic Paradigm*, Power Publications, Sydney.

Guillen, Michael (1995), *Five Equations that Changed the World*, Little, Brown & Co., London.

Gunn, Thom (1982), Clive Wilmer, ed. (1982), *The Occasions of Poetry: Essays in Criticism and Autobiography*, North Point Press, San Francisco.

Hart, Kevin (2004), *The Dark Gaze: Maurice Blanchot and the Sacred*, University of Chicago Press, Chicago.

_____ (1989) *The Trespass of the Sign: Deconstruction, Theology and Philosophy*, Cambridge University Press, Cambridge.

Hawthorn, Jeremy (2000), *A Glossary of Contemporary Literary Theory*, 4th edn., Arnold, London.

Hayles, Katherine N. (1991), *Chaos and Order: Complex Dynamics in Literature and Science*, University of Chicago Press, Chicago.

_____ (1990), *Chaos Bound: Orderly Disorder in Contemporary Literature and Science*, Cornell University Press, New York.

Hejinian, Lyn (1992), *The Cell*, Sun & Moon, Los Angeles.

Henderson, Linda Dalrymple (1983), *The Fourth Dimension & Non-Euclidean Geometry in Modern Art*, Princeton University Press, Princeton.

Herbert, W.N. and Hollis, Matthew, eds. (2000), *Strong Words: Modern Poets on Modern Poetry*, Bloodaxe, Tarset, Northumberland.

Hersh, Reuben (1997), *What Is Mathematics, Really?*, Oxford University Press, New York.

Holquist, Michael, ed. and, with Emerson, Caryl, tr. (1981), *The Dialogic Imagination: Four Essays by M.M. Bakhtin*, University of Texas Press, Austin.

Hubbard, Barbara Burke (1996), *The World According to Wavelets: the story of a mathematical technique in the making*, A.K. Peters, Wellesley, MA.

Hughson, Lois (1977), *Thresholds of Reality: George Santayana and Modernist Poetics*, Kennikat, New York.

Huisman, Rosemary (1998), *The Written Poem: Semiotic Conventions from Old to Modern English*, Cassell, London.

Johnson, Barbara (1980), *The Critical Difference: Essays in the Contemporary Rhetoric of Reading*, Johns Hopkins University Press, Baltimore.

Justice, Donald (1984), *Platonic Scripts*, University of Michigan Press, Ann Arbor.

_____ (1995), *New & Selected Poems*, Knopf, New York.

Karlinsky, Simon (1985), *Marina Tsvetaeva: The Woman, her World and her Poetry*, Cambridge University Press, Cambridge.

Kearney, Richard (1984), *Dialogues with Contemporary Continental Thinkers: The Phenomenological Heritage*, Manchester University Press, Manchester.

Kermode, Frank (1968), *Continuities*, Random House, New York.

_____, ed. (1975), *Selected Prose of T.S. Eliot*, Faber & Faber, London.

Kierkegaard, Søren, tr. Capel, Lee M. (1965), *The Concept of Irony: with constant reference to Socrates*, Indiana University Press, Bloomington.

Kinsella, John, ed. (1999), *Landbridge, Contemporary Australian Poetry*, Fremantle Arts Centre, North Fremantle, Western Australia.

Koestler, Arthur (1964), *The Act of Creation*, The Danube Edition (1969), Hutchinson, London.

Lammon, Martin, ed. (1996), *Written in Water, Written in Stone: Twenty Years of Poets on Poetry*, University of Michigan Press, Ann Arbor.

Larkin, Philip (1983), *Required Writing: Miscellaneous Pieces 1955-1982*, Faber & Faber, London.

Lee, A. Robert, ed. (1996), *The Beat Generation Writers*, Pluto Press, London.

Lehman, David, ed. (1987), *Ecstatic Occasions, Expedient Forms: 65 Leading Contemporary Poets Select and Comment on Their Poems*, Macmillan, New York.

Leitch, Vincent B. (1983), *Deconstructive Criticism: An Advanced Introduction*, Columbia University Press, New York.

Lemon, Lee T. and Reis, Marion J., eds/trs (1965), *Russian Formalist Criticism: Four Essays*, University of Nebraska Press, Lincoln.

Levy, Silvio (1995), *Making Waves, A Guide to the Ideas behind 'Outside In'*, A.K. Peters, Wellesley.

Lindsay, Jack (1927), *William Blake: Creative Will and the Poetic Image*, Richard West, Philadelphia.

MacIntyre, Alasdair (1985), *After Virtue: a Study in Moral Theory*, 2nd edn., Duckworth, London.

Macleish, Archibald (1960), *Poetry and Experience*, Penguin, Harmondsworth.

Mair, Miller (1989), *Between Psychology and Psychotherapy: A Poetics of Experience*, Routledge, London.

Monastyrsky, Michael (1987), tr. James King and Victoria King, *Riemann, Topology, and Physics*, Birkhäuser, Boston.

Motz, Lloyd and Weaver, Jefferson Hane (1993), *The Story of Mathematics*, Plenum, New York.

Nietzsche, Friedrich, tr. Golffing, Francis (1956), *The Birth of Tragedy and The Genealogy of Morals*, Doubleday, New York.

_____ tr. Hollingdale, R.J. (1979), intro. Michael Tanner (1992), *Ecce Homo*, Penguin, London.

Norris, Christopher (1991), *Deconstruction: Theory and Practice*, Routledge, London.

Oremland, Jerome (1997), *The Origins and Psychodynamics of Creativity*, International Universities Press, Madison.

Ostriker, Alicia Suskin (2000), *Dancing at the Devil's Party: Essays on Poetry, Politics, and the Erotic*, University of Michigan Press, Ann Arbor.

Ousby, Ian, ed. (1988), *The Cambridge Guide to Literature in English*, Cambridge University Press, Cambridge.

Paulos, John Allen (1991), *Beyond Numeracy: An Uncommon Dictionary of Mathematics*, Viking, London.

Perkins, George and Perkins, Barbara, eds. (1994), *The American Tradition in Literature*, 8th edn., McGraw-Hill, New York.

Perloff, Marjorie (1991), *Radical Artifice: Writing Poetry in the Age of Media*, University of Chicago Press, Chicago.

Petsinis, Tom (1998), *Naming the Number*, Penguin, Ringwood, Victoria.

Poincaré, Henri (1905), tr. Halsted, George Bruce (1913, this edn. 1958), *The Value of Science*, Dover, New York.

Preminger, Alex and Brogan, T.V.F., eds. (1993), *The New Princeton Encyclopedia of Poetry and Poetics*, Princeton University Press, Princeton.

Ramazani, Jahan (1994), *Poetry of Mourning: The Modern Elegy from Hardy to Heaney*, University of Chicago Press, Chicago.

Rice, Philip and Waugh, Patricia, eds. (1996), *Modern Literary Theory: A Reader*, 3rd edn., Arnold, London.

Rilke, Rainer Maria, tr. Bly, Robert (1981), *Selected Poems of Rainer Maria Rilke*, Harper and Row, New York.

_____ tr. Poulin, A., Jr. (1977), *Duino Elegies and The Sonnets To Orpheus*, Houghton Mifflin Co., Boston.

Roseliep, Raymond (1980), *Listen to Light*, Alembic, Ithaca, New York.

Sacks, Peter (1985), *The English Elegy: Studies in the Genre from Spenser to Yeats*, Johns Hopkins University Press, Baltimore.

Salusinsky, Imre (1987), *Criticism in Society: Interviews*, Methuen, New York.

Sarup, Madan (1988), *An Introductory Guide to Post-structuralism and Postmodernism*, Harvester Wheatsheaf, London.

Serres, Michel (1982), tr. James, Genevieve and Nielson, James (1995), *Genesis*, University of Michigan Press, Ann Arbor.

_____ (1983), tr. McCarren, Felicia (1991), *Rome, The Book of Foundations*, Stanford University Press, Stanford.

_____ (1986), tr. James, Genevieve and Federman, Raymond (1989), *Detachment*, Ohio University Press, Athens.

Sewell, Bill and Stace, Jeanette, eds. (1991), *Balancing on Blue*, The New Zealand Poetry Society, Wellington.

Sim, Stuart (1992), *Beyond Aesthetics: Confrontations with Poststructuralism and Postmodernism*, University of Toronto Press, Toronto.

Simpson, Louis (1986), *The Character of the Poet*, University of Michigan Press, Ann Arbor.

Skovron, Alex (1992), *Sleeve Notes*, Hale & Iremonger, Sydney.

Sontag, Susan (1969), *Styles of Radical Will*, Vintage, London.

Stafford, William (1998), *Crossing Unmarked Snow: Further Views on the Writer's Vocation*, University of Michigan Press, Ann Arbor.

Stevens, Wallace (1951), *The Necessary Angel: Essays on reality and the imagination*, Vintage, New York.

_____, Stevens, Holly, ed. (1971), *The Palm at the End of the Mind: Selected Poems and a Play*, Vintage, New York.

_____, Bates, Milton J., ed. (1989), *Opus Posthumous by Wallace Stevens: Poems, Plays, Prose*, revised edn., Vintage, New York.

Stewart, Ian (1997), *The Magical Maze*, Weidenfeld & Nicolson, London.

Stitt, Peter (1985), *The World's Hieroglyphic Beauty: Five American Poets*, University of Georgia Press, Athens.

Stravinsky, Igor, tr. Knodel, Arthur and Dahl, Ingolf (1947), *Poetics of Music in the form of Six Lessons*, Random House, New York.

Sulfur 20 (Fall 1987), "A Note on *Montemora*, America and the World", pp. 195-197.

Sunday Afternoon (October 14 1999), "Conversations with a Dead Poet", Wearne, Alan, Australian Broadcasting Corporation (television documentary).

The Literary Review, 45.1 (2001), "An Interview with Laurie Duggan", pp. 126-137.

Tranter, John (1977), *Crying in Early Infancy: 100 Sonnets*, Makar, Brisbane.

Wallace-Crabbe (1990), *Poetry and Belief*, University of Tasmania (Occasional Paper, 49), Hobart.

Williamson, Alan (1994), *Eloquence and Mere Life: Essays on the Art of Poetry*, University of Michigan Press, Ann Arbor.

Wilmer, Clive, ed. (1982), *Occasions of Poetry: Essays in Criticism and Autobiography*, expanded edn., North Point Press, San Francisco.

Woolf, Virginia, ed. Woolf, Leonard (1954), *A Writer's Diary: being extracts from the diary of Virginia Woolf*, Harcourt Brace Jovanovich, New York.

Zukofsky, Louis (1981), *Prepositions: The Collected Critical Essays of Louis Zukofsky*, expanded edn., University of California Press, Berkeley.

Lightning Source UK Ltd.
Milton Keynes UK
UKHW021958010222
398052UK00010B/2280